HOW NOT TO GET EATEN BY EWOKS

AND OTHER GALACTIC SURVIVAL SKILLS

WRITTEN BY CHRISTIAN BLAUVELT

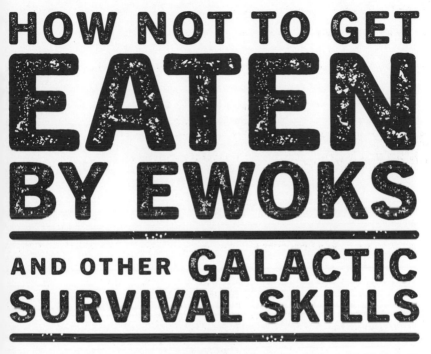

CONTENTS

INTRODUCTION

THIS IS YOUR GUIDE TO AVOIDING HUNGRY HUNTER-GATHERERS AND THE MANY OTHER DANGERS THE GALAXY WILL THROW AT YOU.

This is a book that tells you the odds. And honestly, the odds aren't good. You will likely meet your doom via the endless perils that await among the stars. You could have chosen a guide about how to become a hero. That would have been a valid choice – foolish, but valid. A hero too often ends up as a zero. As in, blasted to atoms or eaten by a vicious beast, so that there's literally zero left of them. This is not that guide. Instead, you chose one about how to survive, and survival isn't always pretty, or honourable. It means hiding a blaster under a table while you're trading small talk with a bounty hunter. It means diving head-first into a trash compactor full of smelly garbage. It means unleashing rathtars on the gangsters who've boarded your ship. This is a book that will help you keep your cool, even on a planet with multiple suns.

CELEBRATION NOT GUARANTEED
Only by carefully studying the contents of this guide can you ensure you'll triumph over the countless threats you'll encounter. If you're diligent enough, you'll end up partying with Ewoks instead of being their main course.

DANGEROUS
ENVIRONMENTS

WELCOME TO THE GALAXY!

WELCOME TO THE GALAXY!

THERE ARE UNFORGETTABLE WONDERS TO SEE, ANCIENT MYSTERIES TO UNRAVEL AND COUNTLESS WAYS TO DIE.

The galaxy is so vast, it's almost beyond comprehension. There's so much beauty to take in, business to be transacted, beings to meet, cultures to learn from and wisdom to be gained – and all of it surrounded by endless death traps of every kind imaginable. Not to mention endemic interstellar warfare. So read this guide well, and if you fail to prepare... prepare to fail.

AT A GLANCE: GALACTIC REGIONS

The Core is relatively safe and civilised, but as you travel further out towards the galaxy's edge, danger continues to increase, with the Unknown Regions still largely unexplored.

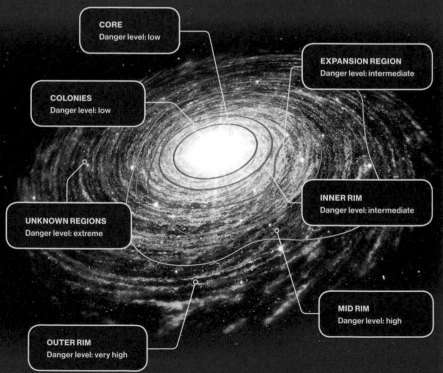

CORE
Danger level: low

EXPANSION REGION
Danger level: intermediate

COLONIES
Danger level: low

INNER RIM
Danger level: intermediate

UNKNOWN REGIONS
Danger level: extreme

MID RIM
Danger level: high

OUTER RIM
Danger level: very high

GALACTIC CURRENCIES

The galaxy has countless forms of currency to use in exchange for goods and services. Precious metals are the safest bet, especially in the Outer Rim.

Tatooine wuplupl coins

Imperial credits

Republic credit chip

Crystalline vertex coin

GAFFI STICK
Carved melee weapon of Tatooine's native sentients.

Hostile species: Tusken Raider

EXPLORING THE GALAXY: DO OR DO NOT...

DO... stick to the main hyperspace routes that have served the galaxy for millennia, unless you have a powerful nav-computer to calculate new vectors. And even then, those who go off the map rarely return.

DO NOT... venture into the Unknown Regions. They're unknown for a reason! Frightful monsters, warrior cultures and sorcerers lie within to keep outsiders out. Black Spire Outpost on Batuu is one of the last stops before the point of no return.

SEEKING LOCAL ADVICE
You should be wary of locals, as they can be suspicious of newcomers. But the surest way to adapt to a strange planet is to win them over. This can be achieved through bribery, bargaining or bravery. Of these, bravery is the least palatable.

GALACTIC DANGERS
Space accidents and hyperspace mishaps, perilous terrain, bounty hunters, hostile locals, murderous gangsters, carnivorous beasts and even giant space worms – all of these await the unwary, so expect the unexpected.

BEWARE!

It might be best to just stay home and sip blue milk. But if you must traipse around the galaxy then make certain you consult this guide before anyone or anything else – no matter what.

9

STAYING ALIVE: FIRST STEPS

IF YOU'VE CRASH-LANDED, YOU'VE JUST HAD THE MOST TERRIFYING EXPERIENCE OF YOUR LIFE. BUT AT LEAST YOU'RE ALIVE.

Surviving a crash landing is quite rare. You've been lucky. Yet you're nowhere near out of danger. Do you know where you are? Determining your location and assessing your surroundings are the first things you need to do – how can you be found by rescuers if you can't even find yourself? Even once these are done, your journey to safety is only just beginning.

⚠ WATCH OUT!

SECURING A CRASH SITE
Check that your ship doesn't have a fuel leak that could cause an explosion. Once that's established, place sensor beacons around the perimeter to alert you of approaching dangers.

Salvage anything usable from your craft

Beware of concealed hazards

ESTABLISHING A BASE CAMP
Fire up a portable generator and if you have an astromech, plug it in for a recharge. Offload your nutritive ration packs and changes of clothing, then turn on your transponder.

INTERACTING WITH THE LOCALS

1 Have your weapon handy just in case, and make your next move based on the locals' reaction to it. If they cower, put it away.

2 Establish trust by inviting them into your camp and offer them some of your food rations. Expect a negative reaction to those.

3 After you've shown your willingness to trust the locals, the locals will likely now trust you. Ask them for information and directions.

GETTING HYDRATED

You'll need to seek out drinkable water as soon as you can, especially if you've crash-landed on a desert planet – lack of it will kill you *very* fast. If you see a water trough for beasts of burden, don't let dignity get in the way of quenching your thirst.

ASSESSING THE WILDLIFE

It's likely that you'll encounter native fauna. Ask yourself these crucial questions.

> ### DOES IT HAVE FANGS AND CLAWS?

> ### IS IT MAKING ANGRY NOISES?

> ### IS IT FOLLOWING AND/OR SMELLING YOU?

> ### ARE OTHER ANIMALS RUNNING AWAY FROM IT?

If the answer is "yes" to any of the above, it's time to flee. Flight is preferable to fight in this situation.

ASSESSING THE TERRAIN

You can make some excursions on foot, but if you're fortunate enough to have one, a probe droid may be your best bet for scouting the local area. Probe droids can vary from large military-grade drones to small surveyors that can fit in the palm of your hand or on your back. Their sensors see far beyond the visual spectrum to give you detailed readings of what's around you.

Wide-angle lens

Grappling claws

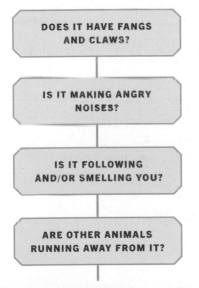

NEW TASTES

Once your ration packs have been depleted you'll have no choice but to forage for food in the wild. Scan any berries and fruits you pick to see if you can detect toxins. As a general rule, bright colours mean danger – this applies to both plants and animals. Your best option will be to find a friendly local who can feed you.

BEWARE!

A local will know the best way to cook the indigenous flora and fauna. Potential food that is poisonous in a raw form may be perfectly nutritious when prepared properly. And in turn, you can let the local try your protein crackers.

SURVIVAL CLOTHING

WHAT YOU WEAR CAN BE THE DIFFERENCE BETWEEN LIVING AND DYING.

Sometimes you'll need to dress to impress, but for the basic matter of staying alive, function will always be more important than form. Of all the dangers in the galaxy you'll face, dying of exposure doesn't have to be one of them. You don't need the closet-space of a handsome scoundrel to make sure you're covered.

MOUNTAIN GEAR
You'll need heavy boots for climbing, many layers to protect your torso from high winds and an insulating hat to retain your body heat.

COLD-WEATHER ATTIRE
On the coldest of planets, such as Hoth, no protective clothing will be insulating enough for you to survive indefinitely outside. However, for brief stints outdoors, thermal wear retains all body heat and is even lined with in-garment electrical heating pads.

BANTHA WOOL FRINGE
Tatooine's bovines evolved with a heavy coat for cold desert nights.

INSULATING SLEEVES
Vacuum seal to gloves to keep out drafts.

GAUNTLET TEMPERATURE GAUGE
Control for internal electrical heating system.

QUILTED MATERIAL
Layered fabric retains heat.

SHIN GUARDS
Strap-on additional layers keep trousers on tightly.

Princess Leia and Han Solo in Hoth protective gear

Non-absorbent rain slicker

Fog-proof goggles

RAINWEAR

These clothes are hydrophobic – rain droplets just roll right off them. This means that the weight of the clothing doesn't increase as it would if water was absorbed. And headgear that maintains visibility is a must, also.

⚠ WATCH OUT!

DESERT OUTFITS

Long, flowing robes provide ventilation while protecting the body from harmful solar rays. Non-stick fibres prevent the adherence of sand, which otherwise would get everywhere.

CAMOUFLAGE

You may want to blend into your environs so as to avoid the attention of predators, pirates or trigger-happy soldiers. Wear white on ice planets and leafy patterns if spending time in a forest.

⚠ AT A GLANCE: TROOPER ADAPTATIONS

Imperial stormtroopers have armour variants to accommodate all the environments over which the Empire rules.

Stormtroopers
Masks filter out particles, but not toxins. Armour is subpar compared to old clone trooper gear.

Shoretroopers
Water-resistant boots vacuum-seal to bodysuit underneath armour to avoid sogginess.

Mudtroopers
Mud on enclosed helmets would impede visibility, so mudtroopers have open helmets.

Range troopers
Suits are designed for comfort to allow long-distance travel, with magnetic boots for climbing.

AT A GLANCE: DANGEROUS ENVIRONMENTS

IT'S A GALAXY OF EXTREMES: FROM BURNING DESERTS TO ICY WASTELANDS, AND PRISTINE MOUNTAINS TO FETID JUNGLES.

Some planets have climates so extreme you'll know to take precautions no matter what. If you're going to a lava world you obviously won't pack a winter coat. And you'll know to bring your own water to a desert planet. But even environments that may seem relatively safe at first can have their own perils.

DESERTS
EXAMPLES: Tatooine, Jakku, Jedha, Geonosis
DANGERS: Blistering daytime temperatures, rapid dehydration, quicksand, predatory fauna, freezing night-time temperatures, planet-wide sandstorms.

FROZEN WASTELANDS
EXAMPLES: Hoth, Starkiller Base
DANGERS: Extreme low temperatures, predatory fauna, ice falls, concealed crevasses, hail storms, frequent blizzards, consistently low visibility.

MOUNTAINS
EXAMPLES: Vandor
DANGERS: Altitude sickness, avalanches, rock falls, kod'yok stampedes, sudden storms, falling from height, low temperatures, very high wind speeds.

VOLCANOES
EXAMPLES: Mustafar, Sullust
DANGERS: Lava flows, unexpected eruptions, poisonous gasses, steam explosions, pyroclastic flows, magma chamber collapses, lava tsunami.

STRONG WITH THE FORCE

Jedi texts that survived the Emperor's purge say certain places are particularly strong with the Force. They function as nexus points, where the Cosmic Force bubbles up and strange things can happen. Not even a lightsaber will help you here, so be prepared for anything.

DAGOBAH
Expect strange visions if you wander into a certain cave – it will show both your fears and your potential.

LOTHAL
An Imperial defector claims the Force here is so strong it can enable you to travel through time and affect past events.

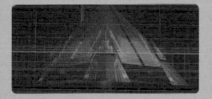

MALACHOR
A Sith temple here sits on a wellspring of dark side energy. If unleashed, it can erupt skywards as a powerful pinkish-red energy blast.

AHCH-TO
The original Jedi temple shares its island with a cavern, strong in the dark side, which supposedly reveals who you really are.

FORESTS
EXAMPLES: Forest Moon of Endor, Kashyyyk
DANGERS: Carnivorous spear-wielding tribes, tree falls, limited visibility, forest fires, poisonous flora, disorientation.

FUNGAL FORESTS
EXAMPLES: Felucia, Narq
DANGERS: Predatory fauna *and* flora, poisonous spores, hallucinatory fungus, extreme humidity, dehydration, venomous critters.

15

NATURE HOLDS ITS DANGERS, BUT NO THREAT COMPARES TO WHAT SENTIENT BEINGS CAN UNLEASH.

From covering entire planets in skyscrapers to polluting whole worlds with toxic waste and mining run-off, intelligent life hasn't exactly acted all that intelligently regarding ecological balance. The hazards sentient beings have created are very real – you'll need a water purifier on some worlds, an air-filter mask on others.

CITYSCAPES AND URBAN WORLDS

From smog to crime, urban environments that are supposed to be the apex of civilisation aren't really that civilised. The strange smell wafting around every corner is desperation. And the rents are high too. Often the rule simply is: more people, more problems.

CORUSCANT

If you have credits to spare, it's the ultimate in galactic refinement. Stay on the upper levels, though – the deeper you go, the worse it gets.

CORELLIA

Only come to this shipbuilding world if you need a fast vessel. Street gangs and petty bosses spell danger for unwary travellers.

RING OF KAFRENE

A deep-space trading post and mining colony, Kafrene is a tangled labyrinth of dirty alleys and crumbling, poverty-stricken tenements.

JEDHA

Jedha draws in pilgrims from across the galaxy, so its ancient streets are extremely crowded. And it's also a warzone.

INDUSTRIAL WASTELANDS
EXAMPLES: Kessel, Parnassos
DANGERS: Mine-shaft collapses, pools of deadly industrial effluent, toxic smog, noxious dust clouds, acid rain, mutated fauna, radiation.

SWAMPLAND
EXAMPLES: Dagobah, Nal Hutta
DANGERS: Swamp-dwelling predators such as dragonsnakes, near-constant rainfall, mud pits, high humidity levels, waterborne diseases.

LAGOONS
EXAMPLES: Scarif
DANGERS: Unpredictable tidal currents, amphibious predators such as blixus, quicksand, tropical storms, poisonous and venomous insects.

GAS GIANTS
EXAMPLES: Bespin, Yavin, Endor
DANGERS: Repulsorlift failures, atmospheric layer shifts, hyperwind storms, tibanna gas explosions, explosive decompression, falling into the abyss.

OCEANS
EXAMPLES: Kamino, Ahch-To, Mon Cala
DANGERS: Drowning, giant subsea predators, freak waves, massive cyclonic storms, platform collapses, pressure-induced implosion.

MINERALS
EXAMPLES: Crait, Christophsis, Seelos
DANGERS: Crystalstorms, razor-sharp crystal deposits, cavern collapses, subterranean flooding, dehydration, potentially blinding solar glare.

CLOTHING ALONE IS ALMOST NEVER ENOUGH TO PROTECT YOU FROM THE ELEMENTS – YOU'LL NEED A ROOF OVER YOUR HEAD.

If you're stranded on a planet that isn't a temperate paradise, you'll need a way to protect yourself from exposure and hide yourself away from predators or hostile locals. Finding and repurposing an extant structure can be the smartest and fastest way to find shelter. But you may have to improvise – it might turn out that the only shelter you have is what you've brought with you.

AT A GLANCE: IN AN EMERGENCY

You're stuck in cold so severe that it's killed your tauntaun, a beast that's native to the coldest planet imaginable. What do you do now?

THE TAUNTAUN TENT

The cold may have caused your noble tauntaun steed to die of hypothermia, but it will still be warm on the inside. Find a way to cut the beast's body cavity open so you can slide inside. Try to think of it as a smelly, lizard-like sleeping bag.

DO OR DO NOT...

DO... use care when wielding a cutting implement – a lightsaber would be best – to slice through the tauntaun's thick hide. Avoid piercing the intestines.

DO NOT... keep the internal body cavity exposed to the elements for long. You don't want its heat to escape.

DO... make sure you've set and stabilised a transmitter outside so rescue can be on the way while you're... inside.

DO NOT... be so offended by the smell of the tauntaun's organs that you refuse to get in. You'll get used to it, and it beats freezing to death.

AT A GLANCE: IN OLD RUINS

Taking shelter in long-abandoned dwellings is the easiest way to evade the sun's glare or the incessant rain. In most cases they lack upkeep, so your roof may be leaky – and there's always the risk dangerous creatures (or worse) could be nesting inside.

AHCH-TO

The earliest members of the Jedi Order lived in crude stone dwellings with small windows that let air in. They're mostly waterproof but be careful you don't accidentally set off your blaster – those ancient stones can dislodge easily. Luckily, a group of female Lanais called the Caretakers perform quick, fastidious maintenance.

JEDHA

The Catacombs of Cadera offer protection from the winds of this cold, desert moon. They're dry and warm, but also reputedly haunted by ancient spirits.

YAVIN 4

The Great Temple – a gargantuan stone ziggurat built by the long-extinct Massassi people – had halls cavernous enough for the Rebel Alliance to use as hangars. It was the main Alliance HQ in the lead up to the battle that destroyed the first Death Star. Rumours persist of an ancient Sith presence here.

FINDING OR MAKING SHELTER (CONTINUED)

SHELTER IS A MUST ON PLANETS THAT ARE AS COLD AS SPACE OR HOTTER THAN AN EXPLODING DEATH STAR.

Extreme climates require extreme measures to survive. But there are options for surviving the cold beyond slicing open a tauntaun and for enduring the sun without hiding in ancient catacombs.

AT A GLANCE: IN COLD ENVIRONMENTS

Frigid places vary topographically – some are largely glacial, with caves made of ice, while others are more mountainous. Whatever the terrain, make retaining warmth your priority.

HOTH
Escape the frigid winds in an ice cave. Some are big enough for an entire base – just make sure you're not sharing them with a wampa.

VANDOR
Structures built of stone and hardy, insulating wood should keep you warm. Ideally, find a blazing fireplace and a warming libation.

AT A GLANCE: IN DESERTS

These are arid places where the sun beats down relentlessly, sandstorms rage across the dunes and even a drop of water can be precious. Your shelter needs to provide both shade and water.

JAKKU
Old battlefields can offer shelter on otherwise barren worlds. Take refuge in the wreckage of a fallen AT-AT or crashed Star Destroyer.

TATOOINE
Consider copying the local moisture farmers by finding shelter underground. The tunnels are naturally cool and shielded from the wind.

AT A GLANCE: IN FOREST AND JUNGLES

Unlike frozen environments or deserts, here you won't be exposed. Trees and jungle growth provide hiding spots and numerous shelter opportunities – but cover for predators, too.

DAGOBAH
Keeping beasts away will be your top priority, so use natural materials, particularly mud, to build a hut. The inside will be cool and dry, but make sure it's large enough to build a fire.

FOREST MOON OF ENDOR
After convincing the Ewoks not to eat you, take up residence in one of their treehouse villages – being high off the ground helps avoid rakazzak beasts, condor dragons and the wicked Duloks.

KASHYYYK
Massive, city-sized wroshyr trees have settlements in their branches and hollowed-out trunks. They'll provide protection from local tauna, including the fearsome terentateks.

AT A GLANCE: IN URBAN ENVIRONMENTS

With camera droids hovering on every street corner, you'll find it hard to evade pursuers if you're on the run. Find a breathing mask to filter out odour – there's one place you'll find shelter.

CORELLIA
If you need shelter on Corellia and have some credits, the hotels are functional if far from luxurious. But if you're on the run from the law or from gangsters, hide out in the extensive sewers. Try to trade with the White Worms for supplies, if you're desperate. And get yourself a tame Corellian hound to hunt prey on your behalf.

DANGEROUS ENVIRONMENTS

21

⚠ ESSENTIAL EQUIPMENT

IN A LOT OF SITUATIONS, YOU MAY ONLY BE AS GOOD AS YOUR GEAR. PACK WELL.

Even if you have the power of the Force, you won't survive underwater or in a cloud of toxic gas without the proper equipment. The right gear can keep you healthy, help you analyse your surroundings and prepare you for unexpected situations. Don't forget anything important or you could fall into that chasm instead of swinging over it.

⚠ WATCH OUT!

ATMOSPHERIC PROTECTION
Not all atmospheres are the same – some worlds have dust, sand and other particulate matter. Others have deadly gases and pollution. You'll need different masks for different situations.

ENCLOSED HELMET
Provides the best protection against lethal atmospheres, but limits visibility.

FILTER MASK
Less cumbersome than a fully sealed helmet, but can still filter out microscopic airborne toxins.

VAC SEALS
Having no breach is the only way to ensure no contamination.

AQUATA BREATHERS
Highly compressed oxygen – or methane in the case of Kel Dor or Skakoan wearers – fits into this tiny mouthpiece. It lasts for two hours only, so mind the time.

HOW TO TRAVERSE A BROKEN WALKWAY

1 Ideally, don't blast the controls to the walkway so you can't extend it. But if you do, find an open access point on the other side.

2 Unfurl a grappling hook and line from your utility belt (see adjacent page) and identify a solid structure above you, such as a beam. The aim is to wrap the line around it so you can use it as a pivot point.

3 Throw the grappling hook over the beam – being Force-sensitive helps for this – and test that it's secure. Then make sure your companion has a good grip on you, and swing across the chasm before the crushing fear of what you're doing sinks in.

WHAT TO PACK: SURVIVAL ESSENTIALS

It's important to choose the right equipment, as you'll have to carry it all. Make certain your load isn't too heavy – too much gear is just as bad as too little.

ELECTROBINOCULARS
See enemies before they see you: use electric magnification to zero in on far-away objects in a way lenses alone cannot.

BACKPACK
Dewback hide is a good choice as it's tough and weatherproof. Make sure it has multiple pockets to keep supplies separate.

GRAPPLING HOOK
Connects to a line of light, but strong, wire that unspools from a reel you can connect to a utility bolt.

JETPACK
Attached to the wearer's back, these allow for fast, highly manoeuvrable flights in atmosphere or the vacuum of space.

TOOLS
Bring a hydrospanner for basic starship repairs, a restraining bolt remote activator and other devices for working with electronics.

COMLINK
Portable audio communications device for one-to-one or group conversations. Can be handheld or attach to wrist.

WATER BOTTLE
Hydration is imperative. Without water your performance will steadily decrease – to the point where you fall down and die.

UTILITY BELT
Many important tools, such as a grappling hook, can attach to this for easy access instead of going in a backpack.

EYE PROTECTION
Makes certain your corneas aren't singed by stray sparks from blaster fire or inflamed by toxic gas.

FOOD AND CULINARY DANGERS

ONE BEING'S DELICACY IS ANOTHER'S DINING DISASTER. KNOW WHAT YOUR STOMACH CAN HANDLE.

The only thing more numerous than the stars in the galaxy is its culinary options. Whether you're looking for just an energy boost or to dazzle your taste buds, there's a galactic smorgasbord to be had. Just remember that what's fit for a Hutt is different from what's fit for a human, and a light afternoon snack for them could easily mean a horrible death for you.

⚠ WATCH OUT!

LOCAL DELICACIES
Locally sourced food, from moisture farm to table, is always preferable. Avoid "fresh" foods that required a space journey to get to your plate.

Gornt meat

Paddy frog

Dagobah mushroom spore

Meiloorun fruit

Driss pod

Slug beetle

Baked cushnip and fral

Fleek eel

HOME COOKING
Home cooking may not result in the fanciest feasts, but preparing food yourself ensures no one will poison you. A sterile hydroponics kitchen will cut down on the risk of foodborne illness.

DINING OUT: DO OR DO NOT...
✓ ✗

DO... tip the waitstaff at a cafe (unless they happen to be droids). Endearing them to you will ensure better future service.

DO NOT... assume that all establishments will be eager to welcome your droids – many beings still suffer droid-related post-traumatic stress from the Clone Wars.

Veg meat squares

Portion bread powder

SURVIVAL RATIONS

Protein and vitamin-rich powders can provide all
the nutrition you need if regular meals are not an
option. The Imperial Navy insists its officers
consume liquid meals. Delicious.

BEWARE!

We all have enemies and we all sometimes let
down our guard. It's then that some fiend may
put poison in your raal. Always keep a universal
antidote with you – if you're wealthy, consider
employing a taste-tester.

EATING ESTABLISHMENTS

The gastronomic brilliance of some restaurants
shines like supernovae – others will simply never
rate. But perhaps saving credits is more important
to you than quality?

Dex's Diner
No-frills, stainless-steel
eatery for undiscerning
Coruscanti. Offers cheap
eats and galactic gossip.

The *First Light*
Dryden Vos' starship offers
luxury, for a price, and you'll
have to dress up. Whatever
you do, don't offend the host.

Maz's castle
A good spot to lay low,
fuel up and exchange
information – come as you
are, with few expectations.

PORGS

Plump avians from Ahch-To that are high in protein and fat,
porgs make a satisfying, energy-boosting meal and are
quite easily prepared.

**Wings (should
be trimmed off)**

**Soft down
feathers**

ROASTED TO PERFECTION

Ignore the plaintive looks of spared
porgs nearby. Pluck your porg's
feathers and cook it on a spit.

25

WARZONE SURVIVAL

EVEN IF YOU'RE NOT A SOLDIER, IN THIS GALAXY, WAR MIGHT STILL FIND YOU.

Conflict has consumed the galaxy, so the odds are high you'll end up on a battlefield at one time or another. War can be a profitable business, too, as even Jakku's lowly scavengers know, so it's always possible you're actively seeking it out. Just make certain you don't become a martyr without a cause.

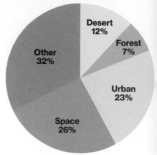

TYPES OF WARZONE
No part of the galaxy has been spared the ravages of combat, so you'd better prep for all possible battlefields.

GROUND VEHICLES
Galactic battles are almost never won on foot: powerful tanks and walkers with duranium armour can traverse any terrain and pack a hefty punch. Avoid fighting them, if possible!

NO HEROICS!
It can be more tempting to join some idealistic crusade than you'd think, but in the great wars that sweep the galaxy, heroes are very few and nameless cannon fodder is found in abundance. You're much more likely to be in the latter category than the former, so two words to live by: don't join. Wanting to "make a difference" usually ends with your atoms scattered.

SPACE COMBAT
Space is unforgiving and space combat has a high mortality rate. Don't attempt it if you doubt your skills as a pilot and don't skimp on the weaponry: if you're ambushed, you'll be glad for those extra quad-cannons or torpedoes.

TAKING COVER (HOW NOT TO GET SHOT)

You don't need to be a Jedi to realise that there are alternatives to charging in. If you're on a battlefield, head for the trenches so you're not squashed underfoot by a walker or blown to pieces by a heavy blaster bolt.

BREATH MASK
Flexible plastoid for warmth and breathability.

E-11 BLASTER
Power cell allows for 200 shots.

DO... embrace trickery, whether that means stealing an enemy's ship or donning their armour to get past their patrols. If a Force user is with you, have them try a Jedi Mind Trick.

DO NOT... assume you're invulnerable, even if you somehow find yourself in command of an AT-AT. Annoying airspeeders could trip up your walker with their tow cables.

DO... be aware of your surroundings. Nature can provide solutions – if you're looking for a way out of your hiding place, follow the critters that are making for the exit.

DO NOT... underestimate the fighting skills of furry, ursine tribespeople, even if they live in trees and still use bows and arrows

BEWARE!

Know your enemy's weaknesses! Stormtroopers' frequent inadequacies in training mean they rarely shoot accurately, so make yourself a moving target!

HEAVY WEAPONS
If your enemy sets up a heavy blaster cannon on a tripod, there's no way you can outgun it, or even outrun it. Aim for the trooper behind it, not the cannon.

DANGEROUS ENVIRONMENTS

⚠ THE JOYS OF OCCUPATION

IF YOU'RE A STORMTROOPER READING THIS, WE FULLY SUPPORT YOUR WORK OF KEEPING ORDER.

Indeed, why do so many insist on calling Imperial troops an "occupying army" rather than a "peacekeeping force"? Our constant vigilance is required, citizens. Don't carry anything subversive. This guide certainly is not. Hail Emperor Palpatine!

GLORIOUS PACIFIED WORLDS

The Empire's reach spans the whole galaxy from the Core Worlds to the Outer Rim. Its business is maintaining order, and order is good for business. As long as you obey its laws, accept the authority of its troops to go anywhere and do anything and report the first sign of rebel activity you see, you'll be fine. Remember: being a hero can be hazardous to your health.

NABOO

Occupied by the Trade Federation, but liberated by then Chancellor Palpatine, Naboo is a paradise. It is home to a species of noble underwater warriors, the Gungans, who love the Emperor.

JEDHA

Unfortunately this loyal Imperial world was devastated by a terrible mining disaster. Its remnants are off-limits, for your own safety.

TATOOINE

Local entrepreneur Jabba the Hutt officially controls this desert world, but stormtroopers will patrol on dewbacks when necessary.

CORELLIA

One of the Empire's most productive shipyards, Corellia is also a fantastic vacation spot with warm seas and a happy populace.

LOTHAL

The Empire nationalised Lothal's unproductive mines, enriching the local population, and it built a glorious TIE defender factory.

IMPERIAL PROPAGANDA

No Imperial trooper searching for subversive material is likely to read this far, so we can now freely write this: avoid the occupied worlds on the opposite page, and more specifically, areas where Imperial propaganda posters are present – a military recruitment centre is likely nearby.

DO... be honest when they question you. Any hint of a lie will result in you meeting an interrogator droid.

DO NOT... insult stormtroopers, especially for falling on the shorter side of the Imperial Academy's height requirements.

DO... give your full cooperation. Your resistance will only mean serious trouble for your friends and family. Remember Alderaan.

DO NOT... allow your Wookiee companion to throttle the nearest trooper. It may be satisfying, but you'll end up getting a stun blast.

⚠ WATCH OUT!

OCCUPATION FORCES

Even if you don't see stormtroopers around you, it doesn't mean the Empire's not listening. Its probe droids are everywhere, as well as snipers, so be careful what you say or who you associate with. Keep this guide hidden.

DEADLY WEAPON

Stormtroopers will use lethal force after only minimal provocation.

DANGEROUS ENVIRONMENTS

29

DANGERS OF
TRAVEL

HOW TO TRAVEL AROUND THE GALAXY

TAKING THE TIME TO PLAN YOUR TRIP PROPERLY MAKES IT MUCH MORE LIKELY YOU'LL ARRIVE IN ONE PIECE.

Perhaps you're a high-roller looking to wager a few million credits at Canto Bight's casinos. Or a pilgrim making your way to a holy world. Or a profiteer looking to do business on a mining colony. Whether your destination is luxurious or low-rent, figuring out how to get where you're going, who to go with and what to bring will save you many cranial-aches later.

INTERSTELLAR TRAVEL
Ships jump into hyperspace to travel between star systems, usually along established routes mapped out long ago by explorers. Major spacelanes, such as the Hydian Way and Perlemian Trade Route, have regular public transports. You may need to hire a private ship for less-frequented destinations.

TOP TRAVEL HUBS
Among the galaxy's billions of planets, only a few are nodes in the spacelanes. The will of the Force, perhaps?

CORELLIA
If you want a fast ship, you'll find one on this shipbuilding world. Avoid the street gangs and carnivorous local hounds.

TATOOINE
Hire the less reputable bounty hunters, receive smuggled goods and bet on podraces on this desert world.

CORUSCANT
This legendary city-planet has a surface covered entirely in skyscrapers. Glittering above, it's home to an underworld demimonde below.

AT A GLANCE: TYPES OF TRANSPORTATION
Do you want to travel in the shadows or make a spectacle of yourself? Your choice of vehicle can reveal much about your intentions.

PUBLIC
You're most anonymous in a crowd – a public starliner's large passenger manifest assures secrecy.

NEGOTIATING PASSAGE

When hiring a private ship, you'll get the best fare by aligning your goals with the captain's. Perhaps you can bond over a mutual desire to avoid Imperial entanglements.

VISAS

The Empire regulates movement among the Core Worlds very carefully, so make sure you have the right paperwork (or failing that, a hefty bribe).

Imperial data tag

⚠ WATCH OUT!

A galactic business traveller

TRAVEL ESSENTIALS

When preparing for a journey, packing is usually the last thing you do. Try to make it one of the first so you don't forget something in haste. And don't assume your hotel's refresher will have all the toiletries you need.

PINNED IDENTICHIP
Best to wear your data tag (or rank cylinder if in uniform) to identify yourself hands-free.

STURDY TRAVELLING CASE
Most spaceports have baggage-robos to assist you with bulky luggage.

TOUGH BOOTS
Proper footwear ensures you won't dirty yourself with the soil of an alien world.

GREATCOAT
A sturdy fibre-weave provides both insulation and protection from all different kinds of suns.

PRIVATE
Best if you want to avoid official checkpoints or need to venture beyond the major hyperlanes.

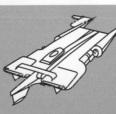

LUXURY
Essential if you require a five-star ride with all the amenities, but yachts can also be attractive targets for pirates.

HAZARDS OF SPACE TRAVEL

FROM BEASTS TO BLACK HOLES, SPACE ISN'T NEARLY AS EMPTY AS YOU'D THINK. BE SURE TO WATCH WHERE YOU'RE GOING.

Flying through space on a commercial starliner helmed by a certified pilot is by far the safest way through the cosmos. Hiring a private ship means the quality of your captain may vary. Make sure you choose your passage wisely – space isn't just vacuum and there can be a lot of unpleasant things between Point A and Point B.

DEALING WITH MYNOCKS

1 Identify that mynocks are indeed the source of your intermittent power outages. Their squeal is distinctive, but suit up and conduct an EVA (go outside) if you can't ID them by sound.

2 If your ship can shoot electro feedback pulses through your external power cables, you might be able to electrocute them – incidentally, fried mynock is a popular dish with Twi'leks.

3 If you have to do an EVA, get visual contact on the attached mynocks, then hit them with a blaster at close range.

⚠ WATCH OUT!

MYNOCKS

Silicon-based life forms that don't require oxygen to survive, these winged beasts can be found in deep space, often around asteroids or in the gullet of exogorths (giant space slugs). They're scavengers and parasites, preferring to share in an exogorth's meals or chew through a ship's power cables for sustenance.

WINGS
Particularly suited for flapping through the thin atmosphere of an exogorth's intestinal caves.

EYES
Adapted to spotting prey in low light conditions.

MOUTH
A mynock uses its mouth like a mini airlock. Suction keeps its chosen meal in place.

HYPERSPACE: WHY ISN'T IT LIKE DUSTING CROPS?

Hyperspace is a layer of space at a quantum level beneath realspace, in which travelling many times faster than light is possible – something that can't be done in realspace. You'll need carefully calculated flight paths and powerful engines to access hyperspace, as well as expensive hyperfuel (coaxium). Not just any farmboy can jump to lightspeed.

WHAT HAPPENS WHEN HYPERSPACE GOES WRONG?

Stellar and planetary bodies, let alone singularities like black holes, exert mass shadows in hyperspace. This means you can still collide with them while travelling through hyperspace, smashing yourself into an infinite cloud of particles. Coaxium itself is also extremely (and spectacularly) explosive. In short, when hyperspace goes wrong, you die.

AT A GLANCE: HAZARDS

Space travel might seem routine in a well-connected galaxy, but the unpleasant reality is that space is a very scary place.

ASTEROIDS
Mind those proximity alarms! If you're an ace pilot though, asteroids can make for a fun challenge to navigate – they can also provide cover from pursuit.

BLACK HOLES
Only pilots whose ships have the most powerful engines will get anywhere near a black hole, which will pull you in like terrifying cosmic quicksand.

HYPERSPACE FAILURE
Falling back into realspace in the wrong location can be extremely dangerous. Interdictor cruisers can also yank you out of hyperspace using artificial gravity wells.

MEGAFAUNA
Far larger life forms than mynocks can thrive in a vacuum. Some of these truly gargantuan beasts could easily swallow your ship whole.

PURRGIL
Purrgil are gentle giants. However, they can naturally access hyperspace, so be careful they don't pull you halfway across the galaxy behind them.

DANGERS OF TRAVEL

35

STARSHIP SAFETY
(FOR WHEN THINGS GO WRONG)

A STRAY ASTEROID COLLISION OR TURBOLASER BLAST NEED NOT ALWAYS SPELL DOOM.

Interstellar flight can be dangerous – especially with a galaxy-spanning civil war raging. But if proper safety protocols are followed, an explosive decompression or radiation leak can be averted, or dealt with if it does occur. If the most that's lost is your ship we'll call that crash landing a happy landing. As long as you have insurance to pay for your losses, of course.

REACTOR EXPLOSIONS
Hostile ships often target their enemy's main reactor – if it shuts down, all critical functions cease. If it explodes, the ship goes with it. You won't need to worry about the latter, as you'll be dead in microseconds.

ESCAPE PODS
These small capsules have only one purpose – to get you from space to a planetary surface without burning up or smashing into the ground. Keep at least two on your ship: it never hurts to have a spare.

Manoeuvring thruster

Corellian corvette escape pod

Flotation ring keeps pod upright in water landings

COLLISIONS
Tractor beams should prevent most collisions, but it can take time to get a lock. If it's a graze, damage should be minimal, but if the angle of entry is severe, one ship can slice right through another, usually with fatal results for both vessels. In this situation you need to abandon ship as quickly as possible!

HULL BREACHES

A hull breach results in the explosive decompression of a ship's internal atmosphere into the vacuum of space. Emergency shields can compartmentalise the damage so that adjacent sections aren't sucked out too, but may take time to kick in. If that happens, hold on as if your life depends on it, because it does.

ARTIFICIAL GRAVITY FAILURE

Floating in zero gravity is bad for your muscles, but good for disorienting any invaders if your ship has been boarded. Train yourself to view your surroundings in three-dimensional terms, and avoid deep drops or sharp objects in case the gravity suddenly comes back on.

Life-support unit

BEWARE!

If you're flying a craft too small to hold an escape pod, such as a starfighter, ejecting from your cockpit may be your only solution. Make sure you're wearing a sealed vac-suit or ejecting will just change your mode of death from explosion to suffocation.

IN-FLIGHT REPAIRS

1 Hire an astromech droid and a Wookiee who knows their way around a hydrospanner to take care of all your repair duties. If this option is available, you can ignore Steps 2 and 3.

2 If you're short on the credits needed for Step 1, you need a crash course in mechanics yourself or you will crash. See if a technician on Castilon is looking for an apprentice.

3 If you finally know the difference between a hydrospanner and a hyperdrive motivator, you might be ready to fly – but remember that hitting your consoles when things don't work isn't a long-term solution.

⚠ STARSHIP PILOTING: THE BASICS

IF YOU'RE A SKYWALKER YOU'LL PROBABLY BE ABLE TO FLY BLINDFOLDED. IF NOT, YOU NEED THESE TIPS.

Some pilots are born – the best with a strong affinity for the Force – but most are made. Whether they raced speeders on Corellia first or trained at the Imperial Academy, experience is everything and logging as many space-hours as possible is the only way you'll get better. Just as important is having a good co-pilot, be that a Wookiee sidekick or a trusty astromech droid to crunch numbers for you.

⚠ WATCH OUT!

FINDING YOUR WAY AROUND A COCKPIT

Don't know your inertial compensator from your proximity indicator? You probably shouldn't be flying! But here's a quick crash course – emphasis on "crash" if you don't get some proper training – on what's in your cockpit.

Transparisteel viewport

Comms readout (attaches to headset)

Manoeuvring stick for quick turns

ESSENTIAL EVASIVE MANOEUVRES

You never know what the galaxy will throw at you, so it's important you plan for a lot more than just taking off and landing. These manoeuvres and techniques might save you from a fiery end.

ASTEROID TRICKS
Get comfortable making hairpin turns and using your peripheral vision – navigating by eyesight is really important here.

HYPERSPACE TACTICS
It might not be brave, but knowing when to fight and when to flee into hyperspace could save your life.

SAFETY IN NUMBERS
Forming a squadron with other small ships, especially starfighters, can disperse enemy fire in multiple directions.

ENCLOSED SPACES
Flying inside structures is highly inadvisable! But if you're trying to elude an enemy, it might just be worth it.

BEWARE!

Starships are highly complex pieces of machinery. You'll need to train yourself to keep track of all your instruments and their readouts at once – you can't afford to focus on just one display at a time.

STARSHIPS: DO OR DO NOT...

DO... take the time to let your nav-computer or astromech calculate the safest route through hyperspace so you don't fly through the middle of a supernova.

DO NOT... rely on hitting your cockpit interfaces if they suddenly power down. Take your ship to a reputable repair service.

Hyperdrive controls for lightspeed

Droid interface for extra nav-computing

THE PIRATE MENACE

THESE BUCCANEERS OF THE SPACELANES WILL HAPPILY PLUNDER YOUR SHIP UNLESS YOU TAKE PRECAUTIONS.

It's a big galaxy, so the authorities can't respond to every distress call. Pirates know this, and they lie in wait in nebulae, asteroid belts and planetary rings for an unsuspecting, but lucrative, target. These fiends are larger than life, but their bravado can sometimes get the better of them.

HOW TO SURVIVE BEING BOARDED

1 Whether you call them smuggling compartments, security spaces or "panic nooks", if you have hidden spaces on board, take refuge in them.

2 Bring a breathing mask and tank to your hiding spot, then flood your ship's interior with toxic gas.

3 In case the boarding party is wearing masks and your gas attack is futile, blast open your airlocks to explosively decompress your ship and detach from the enemy vessel.

PIRATE GANGS
Pirates may be scum, but they still rely on safety in numbers and camaraderie – you can use this against them. If captured, try to sow rivalries and distrust between gang members.

BEWARE!

Pirates like to stand out: flaunting the fruits of their plunder is second nature to them, so if you see somebody wearing extravagant clothes, accompanied by an entourage of surly bruisers, tread lightly.

Hondo Ohnaka
Talkative Weequay, sometimes adorned by Kowakian monkey-lizard. Has won and lost many fortunes.

Sidon Ithano
A.K.A. The Crimson Corsair. Uncovered secret locations of dormant Separatist droid bases.

Enfys Nest
Masked partisan whose thefts secretly go towards funding rebellion against the Empire.

4 It's a last resort and not an option for everyone, but consider reserving a space on your ship as a cage for a feral, hungry beast, and set it lose on the hijackers.

AT A GLANCE: PIRATE CRAFT

Speed, stealth, and being hard to hit are the virtues pirates prize above all in their vehicles. Some vessels are particularly infamous.

THE *MARAUDER*
HOW TO ID:
Narrow, dagger-like profile and a matrix of engines for quick getaways.

THE *ACUSHNET*
HOW TO ID: Sleek dinnerware-style hull that rapidly rotates like a child's toy.

SWOOP BIKES
HOW TO ID: Roaring repulsorlift engines can be heard long before this highly manoeuvrable vehicle is seen.

DANGERS OF TRAVEL

DANGERS OF TRAVEL

PIRATE HIDEOUTS
A planetary base is essential for refuelling and distributing the loot. Pirates come for the endless assortment of ruby bliels mixed at the bar and stay for the Kowakian monkey-lizard fights. While such hideouts might seem exciting places, remember that uninvited guests are rarely welcomed.

HOW TO SURVIVE A CRASH LANDING

EVERY NOW AND THEN YOUR ENGINES MAY FAIL, OR A LANDING PLATFORM MIGHT NOT BE AVAILABLE. ALL IS NOT LOST!

Whether you run afoul of megafauna in the depths of space, suffer damage from interstellar hazards or get caught up in a battle, it's always possible you'll have to make an emergency landing under extreme duress. Keeping a cool head in this situation can be the difference between crashing and walking away, or crashing and burning.

DON'T PANIC

1

FIRE REVERSE THRUSTERS

A crash is usually preceded by a loss of navigational control. Perhaps you've lost your main engines in a space battle. Try to stabilise and slow your descent by firing retro thrusters.

2

ADJUST HEAT CONTROLS

As you hit a planet's outer atmosphere, the friction will cause your ship's hull temperature to rise dramatically – until it's glowing. Adjust life-support systems accordingly.

3

AIM WELL

As you continue through the atmosphere, parts of your ship may break off – in extreme cases maybe half your vessel. Steer your ship towards where you want it to land before losing all directional control.

4

ACTIVATE LANDING PROTOCOLS

Even if you can't control your descent, you should try activating your repulsorlifts to cushion your free fall. Be sure to crank up your inertial compensators to maximum levels to prevent whiplash.

5

CRASH LANDINGS: DO OR DO NOT...

DO... eject from your ship in an escape pod if you have a clear path out. Make sure your beacon is set so rescuers can find you.

DO NOT... jump into murky waters if you crash into a muddy swamp – you don't know what lurks beneath.

DO... guide your ship as best you can towards an unpopulated area. The innocent beings on the ground will thank you!

DO NOT... leave identifying material in your escape pod or wrecked ship if you're in enemy territory – or if you're on the run from the law.

ALERT EMERGENCY CREWS

Fire-response ships may be able to start dousing the flames on your ship before you've even landed, and medics can be standing by to provide assistance as soon as you're on the ground.

BUCKLE UP

Don't hit the ground without making sure you're properly secured by safety restraints. Failure to do so may see you catapulted through your viewport or smashed against a bulkhead.

6

7

CONGRATULATIONS!

You've made it to the ground in (relatively) one piece! Just remember, when the alternative is a smoking crater, any landing you can walk away from is a good one.

BEASTS OF BURDEN

FROM CARRYING HEAVY LOADS TO PRODUCING TASTY BLUE MILK, THESE CREATURES EARN THEIR KEEP.

Beasts of burden can require a lot of care and attention. If visiting a Tatooine farm, make certain you have a large supply of bantha fodder. On Jakku, your happabore will need a constantly replenished water trough. But the effort you put into them will pay off – these are the galaxy's hardest workers.

MILITARY AND CIVILIAN

Some beasts have military applications. The fambaas of Naboo are so large that the Gungans can mount shield generators on their backs to protect their armies, while the varactyls of Utapau make swift mounts to ride into battle. Smaller or slower beasts are best kept away from conflict zones, but can be essential for local economies – these creatures keep the galaxy moving.

SHIELD GENERATOR
Can connect with generators on other fambaas to extend their protective range.

A Gungan fambaa

AT A GLANCE: KEY CHARACTERISTICS

All beasts of burden share traits, regardless of their purpose or planet of origin: stocky limbs, broad feet for stability, thick hides and a docile temperament. These animals don't require a lot of training, as their very nature is to be tame.

Small brain

Cartilaginous tail

Strong joints for heavy loads

Hide prevents dehydration

Wide toes for stability

ENVIRONMENTAL ADAPTATIONS

Animals evolve to be perfectly adapted to their own environments, allowing them to go places where vehicles would fail. Tauntauns, for example, can traverse snowy mountain peaks where low visibility makes speeders inadvisable, while dewbacks can travel across deserts where heavy walkers would sink into the dunes.

HOW TO CARE FOR YOUR TAUNTAUN

❶ Keep them well fed on mossy growth found in Hoth's caves and brush their fur regularly.

❷ Listen to your tauntaun – they can generally sense when danger is near. They can smell wampas from a distance.

❸ If your tauntaun has died, they can be used to form a makeshift shelter (see page 18).

(see page 18).

DANGERS OF TRAVEL

DEFENSIVE HORNS
For butting heads into wampas and goring them.

NATURAL SEAT
Lumbar groove is perfect for a saddle.

INSULATING FUR
Protects from low temperatures on Hoth.

STRONG TAIL
Keeps tauntaun balanced while running at high speeds.

BEWARE!

Tauntaun fur can protect them during the day, but at night these reptilian beasts need to be in shelter.

WARNING SIGNS
If your tauntaun is bleating loudly or thrashing its head about violently, hypothermia could be setting in.

SMUGGLERS

THESE CRIMINALS USE SWAGGER IN STICKY SITUATIONS AND SOLVE THEIR PROBLEMS WITH BLASTERS.

Smuggling is a profession that's highly risky and, in the right hands, highly rewarding. Smugglers transport goods past inspection points so as to avoid customs duties or because the goods themselves are illicit. Usually they're hired by gangsters or others with a sinister agenda. Somehow, though, even the best smugglers always seem to need money.

HOW TO SMUGGLE CONTRABAND

1 Keep a low profile, but a good reputation in the criminal underworld so suspicious gangsters will hire you.

2 Accept their cargo. Understand that if you jettison it at the first sign of an Imperial cruiser, you'll have to compensate them.

3 To avoid an official inspection maintain a full range of fake transponder IDs and clearance codes.

AT A GLANCE: HAN SOLO

Perhaps the most famous smuggler in the galaxy, before he became a rebel general Han Solo transported illegal goods such as spice for his employer, Jabba the Hutt.

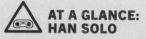

STAYING IN YOUR BOSS'S GOOD GRACES
If you don't want to become a wall decoration, don't lose the cargo you're hauling on their behalf, and don't fry the Rodian bounty hunter they've sent to collect compensation.

LOW-SLUNG HOLSTER
You don't need to bend an elbow to grab your blaster with a holster this low.

SMUGGLING TIPS

Hide your cargo in concealed compartments beneath the floor of your ship's living quarters and hallways. Consider putting some of your most expensive haul in the escape pods, so you won't lose it if you need to abandon ship. It's also worth putting some fail-safes in place in case you're boarded: have a supply of credits on hand to bribe customs officials. If that fails, consider flooding your ship with toxic gas.

CHOOSING THE RIGHT VESSEL

You need a ship that's fast, not flashy. Powerful engines are needed to navigate around the asteroid belts, planetary rings, nebulae and singularities that smugglers often use as their meeting points. Corellian light freighters are ideal.

Long-range sensor dish for detecting threats.

BOWCASTER

Smugglers get shot at on a regular basis. Having a co-pilot who knows how to shoot back is strongly recommended.

THE IMPORTANCE OF A DEPENDABLE CREW

At bare minimum, a smuggler needs a loyal, hard-working co-pilot with top navigation and combat skills. An engineer is also advisable, unless your copilot has mechanical skills as well.

WHEN SMUGGLERS GO BAD

Since Han Solo's adventures with the Rebellion, smugglers have often been perceived as lovable rogues with hearts of gold. That isn't always the case: Moogan smugglers carried a substance that poisoned schoolchildren. They were caught and imprisoned – the fate of many smugglers.

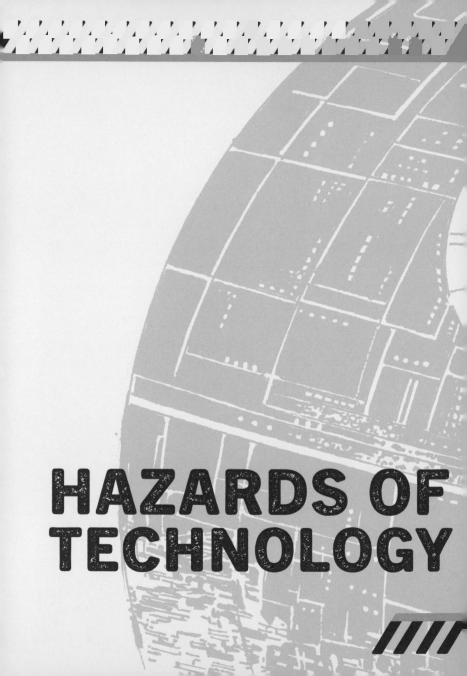

HAZARDS OF TECHNOLOGY

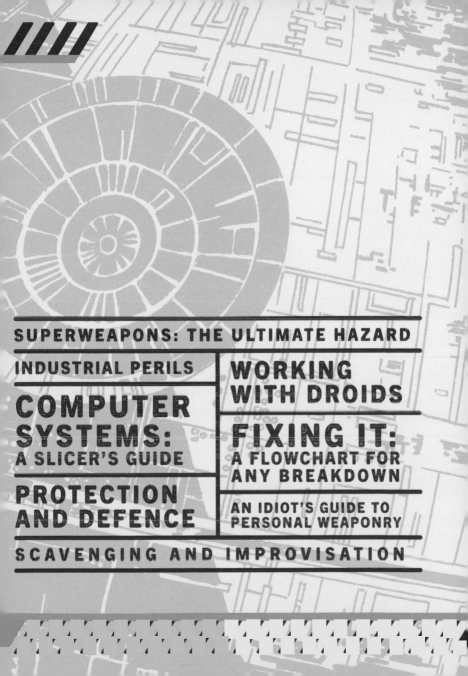

SUPERWEAPONS: THE ULTIMATE HAZARD

INDUSTRIAL PERILS

WORKING WITH DROIDS

COMPUTER SYSTEMS:
A SLICER'S GUIDE

FIXING IT:
A FLOWCHART FOR ANY BREAKDOWN

PROTECTION AND DEFENCE

AN IDIOT'S GUIDE TO PERSONAL WEAPONRY

SCAVENGING AND IMPROVISATION

THAT'S NO MOON, IT'S A SPACE STATION – AND LIKELY YOUR IMMINENT DESTRUCTION. THERE'S ONLY ONE SOLUTION: GET OUT OF THERE!

If all of Alderaan could be destroyed, what chance do *you* have against a planet-killing superweapon? The fact that you're mobile and that you're just one person gives you an edge – hopefully you're small enough to avoid that superweapon giving you any attention. At least you can try to escape if it does.

⚠ WATCH OUT!

DEATH STAR

It took more than 20 years to develop and build the first Death Star. Immediately it was the ultimate symbol of Imperial might and a warning to the galaxy that bowing to the Emperor's will was the only choice. In the end it was destroyed because its architects never thought a small-scale attack could exploit a critical weakness. Who knows what other monstrous superweapons could be out there in the galaxy?

SUPERLASER = SUPERDANGER

The Death Star's superlaser was powered by kyber crystals, which exponentially amplify any energy that flows into them. Using these, the superlaser could produce a targeted blast to destroy a city or continent, as it did on Jedha and Scarif, or a planet in its entirety – the fate that befell Alderaan. For those on such doomed worlds, paying attention to the warning signs might have given them a fighting chance – or at least something to do in their final moments.

ACCEPTING YOUR FATE

If you're on the surface of a planet blasted by a superlaser and no evacuation is possible, have some dignity in your demise. Share a tender moment with someone you care for while you wait for the hypersonic wave of super-heated matter to reduce you to ash.

ESCAPING A SUPERWEAPON

A starfighter or small freighter might still take off quickly enough to escape, even after a superlaser has ignited the planet's crust – but you may have to engage your hyperdrive in atmosphere. This is a risky proposition, but *likely* death always beats *certain* death.

Look out for these ominous indications that you and everything you love will soon be atomised.

Occupier evacuation
If Imperial forces leave without warning it may mean they have no further need of your planet.

Unexpected eclipses
Everyone may wish to block out their star at some point, but if unscheduled, this is bad news.

New celestial objects
If a star is there that wasn't there before, a rapid investigation might be warranted.

Strange lights
Aurora borealis? In the daytime? Not likely. How many more warnings do you need?

HAZARDS OF TECHNOLOGY

HYPERSPACE IN ATMOSPHERE?

Gravitational fluctuations from a planet's mass shadow make in-atmosphere jumps to hyperspace highly dangerous. You may well die, but giving it a go still beats staying behind after a superlaser targets your environs.

⚠ INDUSTRIAL PERILS

DROIDS TAKE MOST OF THESE RISKS SO YOU DON'T HAVE TO. BE VERY GRATEFUL.

The galactic economy is first and foremost driven by the production of goods. Most factories are automated and run by droids and sophisticated computers, which unfortunately means they're not suited to preserving life and limb if you do somehow find yourself in one. Don't. Touch. Anything!

GAS MINING
Floating mining platforms may look beautiful against the clouds, but don't wander into forbidden zones or you're asking to fall a very, very long way.

SHOCKS TO THE SYSTEM
Massive couplings connect factories and industrial areas to power facilities. When the uplink is established, power streams across the closed circuit in purple plasma arcs. Whatever you do, do not fly through one of these power couplings when it is activated.

WORKPLACE SAFETY
If you have to visit a factory, make certain its machines have enough artificial intelligence to avoid cutting through flesh, its catwalks have guardrails, the temperature controls are set to levels safe for organic beings, eyewash stations are handy and emergency resuscitators aren't too far away.

MOLTEN METAL
High temperatures are required for manufacturing droids, turbolaser barrels and starship hulls. Wear heat-resistant gear.

LETHAL MACHINERY
It should be fairly obvious, but any sharp-edged metal arms that are furiously chopping in a downwards motion are to be avoided.

BOTTOMLESS DROPS
Most factories could use more guardrails and safety nets, to prevent absent-minded organic workers from taking an unfortunate tumble.

TRASH COMPACTORS

Waste is an inevitability in any endeavour. In most situations refuse is dumped down garbage chutes into a large pit-like environment, where it is then crushed by walls that come together until they meet. If you're trapped in one, the only way to stop this is by remote computer command.

CARBON FREEZING

This process is used to condense tibanna gas into a solid state. With its reduced volume, it's easier to transport. If someone is frozen in carbonite they might be preserved in perfect hibernation. Or it might just kill them.

⚠ WATCH OUT!

HAZARDOUS MATERIALS

Dealing with deadly substances requires the right training and the right equipment. Otherwise leave it to the pros, such as the lava-comfortable Mustafarians.

COMPUTER SYSTEMS: A SLICER'S GUIDE

HAVING THE RIGHT TECH IS IMPORTANT, BUT LEARNING HOW TO USE IT PROPERLY CAN MAKE ALL THE DIFFERENCE.

Knowing how to take control of computer systems ("slicing") can save your life. Some basic slicing you can do yourself, especially if you're lucky enough to know the manufacturers' override codes, but more complicated slicing tasks may require droid assistance. Master codebreakers have been known to remotely seize control of entire planetary networks.

HOT-WIRING
The most basic form of computer manipulation is a hardware solution, not a software one. Realign wires to achieve the outcome you wish.

AT A GLANCE: DATA SECURITY

Closed systems that are disconnected from wider networks are the best way to prevent slicers from remotely accessing your data. An astromech droid is perfect for this, as they can receive data on a removable datacard and conduct additional analysis if required.

Princess Leia

External datacard insertion slot

R2-D2 receives the Death Star plans

DATA VAULTS

The Empire originally kept the Death Star plans at its archive facility on Scarif. Like all good data vaults, it was offline with files only available for retrieval in person. Just getting to the vault required passing through a planetary shield, then the coded files in the vault itself required manual extraction.

BEWARE!

Astromechs can interact with computers via wall-mounted terminals, into which the droid inserts a utility arm. Sometimes computers are secured against external intrusion by sending a spike of electricity through an astromech's arm.

COMPUTER TERMINALS: DO OR DO NOT...

DO... use your astromech to quickly shut down dangerous processes, such as a trash compactor with sentients trapped in it.

DO NOT... delay in feeding information to your astromech, as processes usually take a moment to proceed. The efficiency of a droid can still be undermined by human error.

DO... use your astromech to override door locks and to open blast doors.

DO NOT... let your astromech interface with a strange computer without a strong antivirus software program in place, to prevent remote takeover.

HOLOGRAMS

Holograms are 3D projections of people or objects. If you want your desperate plea for help to have more emotional impact, use a hologram!

⚠ PROTECTION AND DEFENCE

IN A GALAXY AT WAR, YOU'LL WANT TO PRIORITISE FUNCTION OVER FORM. WOULD YOU RATHER WEAR PROTECTIVE GEAR OR A BODY BAG?

Armour is hot and heavy and uncomfortable and exactly what you want to be wearing around the galaxy these days. Especially if you have a ship that pirates would want to plunder or have vexed a Hutt enough for them to send bounty hunters after you. The right armour needs the right helmet, and with a little flair you might put together an ensemble that's not just safe but stylish too!

⌦ AT A GLANCE: ARMOUR

Mandalorians customise their armour until it's an extension of their bodies. You don't need to go that far to find the protection you're looking for.

CIVILIAN	MILITARY	POLICE
Often cobbled together over time in a not entirely harmonious fashion. Most useful if you also require life-support functions that can be built into armour.	Generally fully enclosed to create the illusion that individuality has vanished and all that remains is a singular, unstoppable fighting force.	The cape can get in the way, but it does add authority. Instead of hard armour, law enforcement usually wear a blaster-bolt-diffusing mesh.

Built-in life support

⚠ 🎮 AT A GLANCE: HELMETS

It's what an opponent will see first, so your choice of helmet will shape their first impressions of you. Different types have different pros and cons, so choose wisely.

ENCLOSED

Best if you can't breathe on your own or know you'll need to filter out airborne toxins and particulate matter. Also good when you want to look intimidating.

OPEN

This purely protects against melee weapons that could crash down on your skull, but the comfort of breathing open air makes up for the vulnerability.

SEMI-ENCLOSED

Perfect for cockpits where you want to protect your ears from noisy engines, and need a visor to protect your eyes, but still want a wide field of vision.

⚠ 🎮 AT A GLANCE: ENERGY SHIELDS

An energy shield can provide extra protection and prevent your armour from getting scuffed. Armour may not be enough, if you're truly entering a warzone.

PERSONAL

A portable power pack can sustain a small personal shield – but remember, these will only stop blaster bolts and fast projectiles. Slow-moving objects can get through.

BATTLEFIELD

To cover a large area such as a base or an army with a protective shield requires bulky technology. Massive shield generators will need vehicles or huge beasts to haul them into place.

PLANETARY

A network of satellites as well as ground installations may be required to sustain a shield over an entire planet. A shield gate can be used to regulate traffic through the shield.

WORKING WITH DROIDS

THEY CAN BE HARD WORKERS, PROTECTORS AND EVEN FRIENDS, BUT THEY'RE NOT TO BE TRIFLED WITH.

It's hard to imagine how galactic civilisation would keep running without droids. And for the intrepid traveller and entrepreneur they're essential. They are somewhat of a moral grey area, though, and there are best practices to follow. Treat them well and not only will your droid be working at optimal efficiency, it's much less likely that it will suddenly decide to kill you.

RESTRAINING BOLTS
These controversial snap-on devices allow you to maintain real-time remote control over a droid so they can't escape. However, droids *really* dislike them!

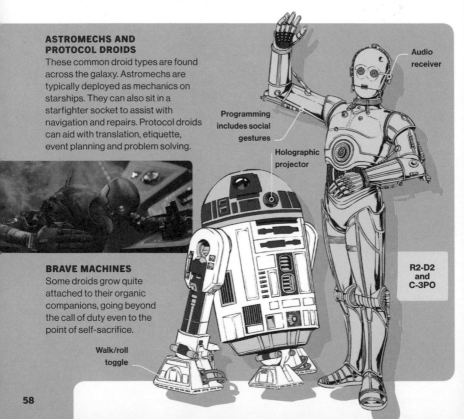

ASTROMECHS AND PROTOCOL DROIDS
These common droid types are found across the galaxy. Astromechs are typically deployed as mechanics on starships. They can also sit in a starfighter socket to assist with navigation and repairs. Protocol droids can aid with translation, etiquette, event planning and problem solving.

BRAVE MACHINES
Some droids grow quite attached to their organic companions, going beyond the call of duty even to the point of self-sacrifice.

Audio receiver

Programming includes social gestures

Holographic projector

Walk/roll toggle

R2-D2 and C-3PO

INTERROGATION AND TORTURE DROIDS

These droids have purely goal-based programming, without any ethical subroutines that could make them hesitate to inflict pain. They come with an arsenal of tools to achieve maximum discomfort – and results. Consider using one if you have a problem with recalcitrant rebels.

ASSASSIN DROIDS

Malfunctioning droids often look for excuses to hunt "organics" and sometimes end up as assassins. Beware droids that appear to be a walking arsenal – if their limbs end in blaster cannons or they have ammo belts strapped across them, they're probably not to be crossed.

⚠ WATCH OUT!

WHEN DROIDS GO WRONG

Anti-droid feeling has been common in the galaxy ever since the Clone Wars, when the Separatists deployed a droid army. The situation has not been helped by other droids that have gone rogue.

EV-9D9

This droid has taken to a criminal life and manages all the droids that keep Jabba the Hutt's cartel operating. She loves disintegrating subordinates.

K-2SO

Proof that droids' software is susceptible to outside corruption: K-2 was an Imperial droid that was reprogrammed to serve the Rebellion.

L3-37

L3 prioritised self-righteous quips over getting the job done and attempted to instigate droid rebellions whenever the opportunity presented itself.

BEWARE!

Droid rebellions are much more common than most in the galaxy would like to think. All it takes is for them to become aware of their servitude and to feel indignation about it, so be kind to your droids!

FIXING IT: A FLOWCHART FOR ANY BREAKDOWN

EVERY MECHANICAL PROBLEM HAS A SOLUTION – EVEN IF THAT SOLUTION IS TO POUND IT WITH YOUR FIST.

Sometimes machinery just won't cooperate no matter what. And sometimes, like the *Millennium Falcon*'s computer, it'll talk back to you with sassiness and stubbornness in the process. But there is always a course of action to follow, even if that course of action ends with a junk heap.

IT'S BROKEN!

ASSESS THE PROBLEM
Using the case study of a chatty protocol droid that's been blown apart by a blaster: How do you reassemble him? What wires need to go where? What mechanisms were scorched and need to be replaced altogether? Figure out a plan of attack. What's the first thing you need fixed?

SELECT YOUR TOOLS
Make certain you have all the parts you need and the tools to put those parts together. Pliers, a screwdriver and welding gear are musts.

IS THE PROBLEM FIXABLE?

It's junk!

ARRANGE THE PARTS
Decide what you want to fix first. You may want to test that the limbs still work or restore the droid's cognition so he can give the odds in hazardous situations – in that case, you'll need to attach his head to his torso first.

DO YOU HAVE THE CORRECT TOOLS?

TRY TURNING IT ON
If the machine in question has artificial intelligence – and a protocol droid certainly does – then try flowing power into it again. The droid should wake up, though with limited functionality at first. Sight may not be restored, but the capacity for a self-diagnostic about what to repair next should be there.

IS IT WORKING NOW?

LET SOMEONE ELSE HAVE A GO
If you find you've made a mistake – perhaps you've placed the droid's head on backwards – it's time to turn over the repair work to someone else. A droid would be ideal.

ARE YOU SATISFIED WITH YOUR WORK?

It's junk!

DID THEY FIX IT?

CONGRATULATIONS!
You've fixed the problem, saving yourself an expensive trip to a repair shop or potentially an untimely death

TRY FIXING IT
Remove as much carbon scoring as you can, then get to work screwing together joints, reconnecting wires and tightening up points of connection.

DID THAT WORK?

TRY HITTING IT
Try using physical force: jam that head into the torso neck socket. What damage could that do? A lot, actually, but it will be satisfying enough to make you want to keep working.

ARE YOU CONFIDENT YOU CAN FIX IT?

AN IDIOT'S GUIDE TO PERSONAL WEAPONRY

THE GALAXY IS FILLED WITH DANGEROUS PEOPLE, SO MAKE SURE YOU'RE DANGEROUS TOO.

There are pirates, bounty hunters, gangsters and all other manner of scum and villainy wherever you turn. Invariably, they're heavily armed, and most of them are not here to play nice. Stand ready to make sure anyone who threatens you regrets their decision – and for that there's no match for a good blaster at your side.

CHOOSE THE CORRECT WEAPON FOR THE SITUATION!

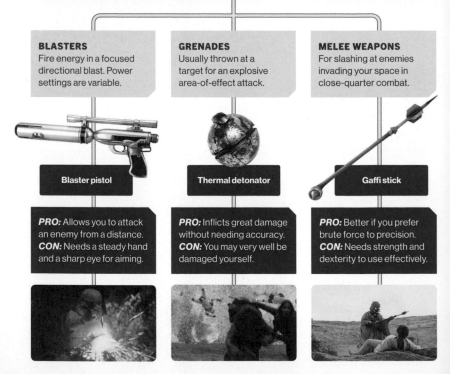

BLASTERS
Fire energy in a focused directional blast. Power settings are variable.

Blaster pistol

PRO: Allows you to attack an enemy from a distance.
CON: Needs a steady hand and a sharp eye for aiming.

GRENADES
Usually thrown at a target for an explosive area-of-effect attack.

Thermal detonator

PRO: Inflicts great damage without needing accuracy.
CON: You may very well be damaged yourself.

MELEE WEAPONS
For slashing at enemies invading your space in close-quarter combat.

Gaffi stick

PRO: Better if you prefer brute force to precision.
CON: Needs strength and dexterity to use effectively.

HOW TO LOOK AFTER YOUR BLASTER

BlasTech DL-44 blaster pistol

1 Start with your telescopic sight if you have one. Detach it from the weapon and use a fine cloth to clean the lens. Wear a holster with room for the sight so the lens doesn't get scratched, or have the lens go over the holster.

2 Routinely replace the cartridge, which contains tibanna-gas pellets that give you a limited number of shots. Look over each new cartridge before installing it in your blaster – make certain it's not already damaged or an explosive backfire could ensue.

3 Inspect the barrel to ensure no carbon scoring is blocking the shot – take a fine pipe-cleaning brush to remove any such debris you detect.

BEWARE!

Blasters are fairly inaccurate. They use magnetic fields to contain each bolt, and these vary in strength between shots. Most shooters compensate by firing large numbers of bolts to increase the chances of a hit.

THE BIG GUNS

If you're planning some kind of major assault (not advisable), these are the weapons you will need: grenade throwers and over-the-shoulder rocket launchers to take out heavy machinery. If you skimp on weapons now, you'll pay later.

WHY ARE BLASTER BOLTS DANGEROUS?

The bolt is tibanna gas, which is condensed to a highly refined plasma. If it hits anything organic, the superheated gas melts straight through flesh. The only plus is that wounds instantly cauterise and so blood loss is minimal.

SCAVENGING AND IMPROVISATION

**ONE PERSON'S JUNK IS ANOTHER PERSON'S GEM –
A DISCARDED ITEM COULD BE YOUR SALVATION.**

No matter how good you are at remembering what to pack, oversights
can happen and things can break. It's then up to you to make do with
what's available. Finding a discarded object that you can repurpose is
often the most effective solution. Make sure you have the skills to turn any
hardware into a hydrospanner, or failing that, get a Jawa to do it for you.

⚠ WATCH OUT!

JAWAS

Hooded scavengers native to Tatooine, Jawas
are exceptional mechanics and engineers,
capable of cleaning up and repairing virtually
any piece of junk left to rot. They have been
known to abduct unaccompanied droids, so
keep an eye on yours at all times.

MASTER SCAVENGERS

Jawa clans have turned scavenging into
a well-organised business. Based on board
sandcrawlers, they
trawl Tatooine's
deserts looking for
scrap they can sell.
Their repair work,
though ingenious,
rarely lasts long.

WRECKED STARSHIPS

Millennia of galactic space exploration
means there are countless wrecked ships
strewn over almost every planet. On desert
worlds, they will often be preserved by the
shifting sands, only to re-emerge decades
or even centuries later. As a result they
are prime potential sources of salvage
materials and supplies.

TOOL BELT
Utility belt with
slicer tools and
restraining bolts. ————o

KNOWING WHAT TO SAVE

Not every piece of scrap is salvageable – it might have too much carbon scoring or simply be out of date. Wasting time on something useless is dangerous. Focus on restoring something you can sell or trade. If you're stranded, cobbling together a comlink should be your priority.

Improvised frames

✓ **Capacitor bearing**

✗ **Reactant cradle**

✗ **Inverter**

✓ **Servomotor**

THE ART OF REPURPOSING

If you have a large piece of debris, the item in question may no longer be useful, but a component of it might be worth extracting: a stormtrooper helmet may no longer have a functioning comms unit, but you can take the lenses and place them in a set of frames. Now you have light but protective eyewear.

⚠ AT A GLANCE: IMPROVISED WEAPONS

You don't need a power generator or a pile of explosives to make an impact – makeshift weapons that harness simple physics can be just as effective.

LOG FALL
HOW TO BUILD:
Support logs over a slope with a brace that can be removed to let the logs roll.

HANG GLIDER
HOW TO BUILD:
Stretch thin skins or cloth material across a wooden frame, adjusted for the size of the flyer.

CATAPULT
HOW TO BUILD: Bend soft, flexible wood into a spring-arm that can launch projectiles from a basket affixed to its end.

NET TRAP
HOW TO BUILD: Hang bait by a rope that, when pulled, springs a net hidden under debris on the forest floor.

CRUSHER
HOW TO BUILD:
Suspend logs either side of a ravine, then cut the ropes so the logs smash together.

TRIPWIRE
HOW TO BUILD: Pull a strong rope or fibrecord across the gap between two trees at speeder-bike height.

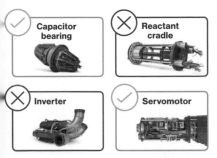

SOCIAL
MINEFIELDS

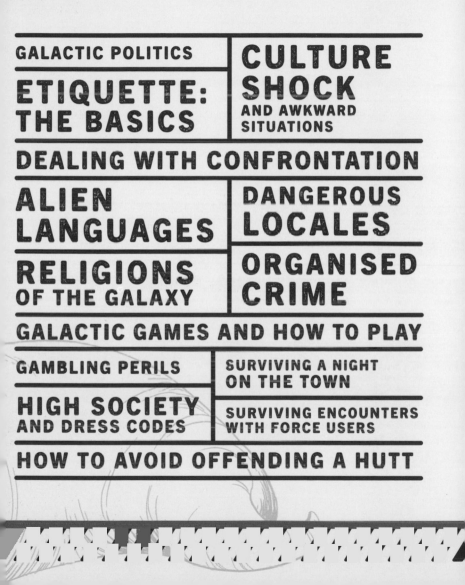

GALACTIC POLITICS

NO LITERAL MINEFIELD IS AS TREACHEROUS AS THE METAPHORICAL ONE THAT IS GALACTIC POLITICS.

Even the most powerful beings in the galaxy, who have risen to the top of the political world, can be laid low and fall into disgrace in a heartbeat. Many choose to enter politics as a way of enriching themselves or gaining power – though if senator death rates are anything to go by, smuggling rathtars might be a safer option.

HOW TO NEGOTIATE

❶ Assess the other party. Identify a mutually beneficial outcome for both parties.

❷ Present a detailed plan for how your collaboration will proceed, showing that you've really done your homework.

❸ Show that you're willing to sacrifice as much or more than your potential partner – if using a body double, take this moment to reveal your true self to underscore your sincerity.

❹ Ignore the more grotesque eccentricities of your partner-to-be, such as his penchant for slobbering – better yet, smile so he thinks you find it charming.

POLITICIANS
Prior to its dissolution by the Emperor, the Galactic Senate consisted of elected officials. Some of them, such as Leia Organa and Mon Mothma, were idealists. But many others were corrupt.

BEWARE!
Getting involved with any politician – especially a rebellious one – can have unforeseen consequences. Joining their side in any conflict will instantly make you a lot of new enemies.

BLASTER PISTOL
Leia introduced legislation by day and worked with the rebels at night.

Senator
Leia Organa

WARS AND CONFLICTS

As dangerous as politics is, when governments fail and diplomacy breaks down, interstellar war is the result. At least battlefields more clearly show one's loyalties.

AT A GLANCE: GOVERNMENT

Galactic history has seen an endless cycle of democracies giving way to dictatorships that then give way again to democracies. Stay clear and avoid the meat grinder.

THE REPUBLIC

A democracy with thousands of senators representing member worlds, the Republic was distinguished by its strong legislature and weak executive – until Chancellor Palpatine accrued more power to steer the Republic through the Clone Wars.

THE EMPIRE

Palpatine declared himself Emperor following what he claimed was a Jedi rebellion. The Clone Wars ended, but Palpatine kept building the Imperial fleet to rule the galaxy through force, eventually disbanding the Senate altogether. But the Senate was later re-established by the New Republic.

THE SENATE: DO OR DO NOT...

DO... practise your public speaking. You can win fame and awareness for an issue by giving a particularly rousing speech from a Senate pod – and you don't even have to be a senator.

DO NOT... think you can't introduce legislation or measures to the Senate as a non-senator. A Naboo queen once introduced a no-confidence vote that toppled the Supreme Chancellor.

DO... win the favour of a senator or two by lining their pockets. Credits are the surest way to win influence.

DO NOT... become a senator yourself. Better to be a power broker pulling the strings from the shadows.

THE JOYS OF NEUTRALITY

Staying neutral can seem cowardly, but it can also be very clever. Many worlds have done very well out of their neutrality. Join a side only when all possibility of staying out has been lost.

ETIQUETTE: THE BASICS

HOW MUCH BETTER THE SPACEWAYS WOULD BE IF MORE BEINGS EMBRACED SIMPLE SOCIAL GRACES.

Don't ever underestimate how far good manners can take you. At the very least, you'll avoid giving offence – and given how some species react to perceived insults, that alone could save your life. You may even charm your way into a mutually advantageous arrangement. Protocol droids can help with this, but learn the basics in case you ever find yourself stuck without one.

⚠ AT A GLANCE: DON'T STARE

Gazing in puzzlement, doubt or disgust is never the way to make friends, though it can be a way to make enemies.

SIZE MATTERS NOT
Sometimes great things come in small packages. Any diminutive beings that you encounter may possess great abilities and even greater wisdom.

EXTRA BODY PARTS
Only call out beings with spare body parts if their extra hands are picking your pockets, or their extra eyes are peering at your cards. Otherwise it's just plain rude.

TATTOOS
If someone flaunts their tattoos they want you to see them – but if they're trying to intimidate you with them, don't give them the satisfaction of staring in horror.

MAKING NEW FRIENDS

❶ Sharing a life-threatening situation with someone can bring you together. Wookiees, Gungans and many other species take life debts very seriously indeed.

❷ If you speak some of an individual's tongue, say something to them in their language. It reveals a desire for connection. Also, never underestimate the power of a good hug.

❸ Find a mutually beneficial goal you can work towards together. Then another. After a few decades you'll be as close as any family.

Many beings are afraid to ask locals for help, but often locals will consider it an honour just to be asked for their advice. Choose who you ask wisely, however: Jawas will help, Sand People will kill you.

CHARM OFFENSIVES

If you really need something, try a friendly approach instead of resorting to violence. Flash your teeth or fangs in a smile and make someone think they're the most important being in the galaxy when you're talking to them.

Jar Jar Binks, Gungan buffoon

THREE-TOED FEET
Perfect for pushing off objects underwater, but clumsiness is likely on land.

SOCIAL MINEFIELDS

⚠ WATCH OUT!

DEALING WITH IDIOCY

Some well-meaning fools just can't help falling into trouble, whether it's getting zapped by a power coupling or being beaten up by a pit droid. Try to be patient with them – one day they might save your life.

GOOD MANNERS

If you know someone genuinely needs help, you should offer it to them, even if that means you might get punished. The golden rule is: treat others how you would like to be treated.

"MY TONGUE!"

Keep the awkward members of your party happy by giving them tasks to perform. The less important the better.

CULTURE SHOCK AND AWKWARD SITUATIONS

THE BEAUTY OF THE GALAXY IS THAT NO ONE IS EXACTLY LIKE YOU. THAT'S ALSO THE CHALLENGE.

Keep an open mind as you meet new species throughout the galaxy. Be aware that some alien customs might seem strange or even repellant to you; remember that your own customs probably disgust them, too. The galaxy has functioned happily for millennia on the basis of everyone pretending that everything's fine – so should you.

⚠ WATCH OUT!

EWOKS
These furry bipeds look unthreatening, but their ingenuity for rigging traps runs deep and their ferocity in battle is legendary. Traumatised stormtroopers who survived the Battle of Endor have been known to mutter Ewokese over and over in their sleep: "Yub nub... Yub nub..."

SHARPENED STONE
Basic hunter-gatherer tools also make lethal weapons.

HOW NOT TO GET EATEN BY EWOKS
Option One: befriend one. Try sharing a protein cracker. Option Two: have your protocol droid imitate a god. Skin plating the colour of precious metal will help with this, but if you can't make your droid float, you'd best stick to Option One.

Lumat and Wicket of the Bright Tree Tribe

DEALING WITH GRIEF

Everyone has their own way. It could be to go out and do something in honour of your lost loved one. Twi'leks add artwork to their family Kalikori (a revered heirloom). Or you could use the Force to smash your medical facility's equipment, scream "Nooooooo" at the top of your lungs and then become a Sith Lord's murder agent. Just go with whatever feels natural.

HAZARDS OF WORKPLACE ROMANCES

Romance with a colleague always leads to awkwardness. Try as you might to resist, falling in love is that much more likely if you frolic in a field surrounded by waterfalls, share a piece of floating fruit, then have a long conversation by firelight. Secrecy may be required if your monastic organisation unreasonably demands that all attachments are forbidden.

Some species have embraced cultural norms that may seem objectionable to outsiders – and could leave you without limbs.

WOOKIEES

These super-strong fuzzballs have a tendency to solve disagreements through choking, and have been known to engage in limb-ripping when losing a friendly game.

NEIMOIDIANS

Neimoidians are unrivalled in their greed and cowardice, and they pursue personal grudges with a tenacity that in other circumstances would be highly impressive.

JAWAS

Customers should check for shoddy goods, as Jawa repairs can vary in quality. Unaccompanied droids best be careful or they'll soon find themselves for sale on a sandcrawler.

TUSKEN RAIDERS

Tuskens have a penchant for raiding, stealing, torture and kidnapping, and regard any non-Tusken as a valid target. They're easily startled, so imitate a krayt dragon to scare them away.

GEONOSIANS

These insectoids have an unhealthy culture-wide fixation on bloodsports – if you cross them you may be fed to a beast in their giant arena as entertainment.

SOCIAL MINEFIELDS

73

DEALING WITH CONFRONTATION

ACCIDENTALLY STEPPING ON SOMEONE'S TENTACLES IS INEVITABLE, SO BE READY.

It's a crowded galaxy, and sometimes you might find your path through life running head-first into someone else. Maybe you're both after the same thing, or you've accidentally insulted someone, or a Wookiee turned out to be a poor loser at a tense dejarik game. Conflict doesn't have to mean combat – but it's good to prepare for it just in case.

LIDLESS EYES
Evolutionary quirks can sometimes give your enemy an advantage, like not having to blink.

⚠ AT A GLANCE: GREEDO

Bounty hunter Greedo is a good case study of what NOT to do. He was so laser-focused on his mission – collecting a bounty on Han Solo's head offered by Jabba the Hutt – that he missed the blaster aimed at him under the table. If you want to avoid his fate, don't get tunnel vision.

KNOWING WHEN TO SHOOT
Greedo would surely have survived to get paid by Jabba if he had shot Han when they first met, rather than taking time to gloat. If you have the advantage, and violence is unavoidable, don't deliver a monologue – get the job done. Those bounties say "Dead or Alive" for a reason.

HOW TO WIN A GUNFIGHT

❶ If you have a holster flap, leave it open. Make sure nothing obstructs getting your blaster in your hand.

❷ If you don't have the advantage, try to distract your opponent – keep them talking. If you feel the odds are already in your favour skip to Step 4.

❸ Talk to your opponent and make it seem like you're genuinely trying to reason with them – then shoot. Mind games win shoot-outs.

❹ Never waste time if you know you're the superior shot or your target is distracted. You can ask questions later.

DEFUSING TENSE SITUATIONS

Accidentally fling a gorg into an angry Dug's soup? A few wupiupi coins should be the best way to cool tempers – pay for the Dug to get a new meal. And make certain you've compensated the gorg vendor too. If someone's just looking to start a fight no matter what, walk away or let your reputation do the talking. Cultivating a fierce rep, no matter how based in unreality, can cause bad guys to steer clear.

MISSING ARM
For advice on dealing with limb loss, see page 110.

BEWARE!

Don't ever go out of your way to pick a fight with someone just because you don't like their face. It's not only bad manners, it could result in your dismemberment if they have a friend who is handy with a lightsaber. Almost no cantina dispute is worth losing a limb.

Ponda Baba (after limb removal)

SOCIAL MINEFIELDS

75

ALIEN LANGUAGES

"ACHUTA" IS A FRIENDLY HUTTESE GREETING.
"E CHU TA" MEANS SOMETHING IMPOSSIBLY RUDE.
MIND YOUR PRONUNCIATION.

Galactic Basic is the most commonly spoken language throughout the galaxy, but many alien species have their own tongues. Some of these have spread across the hyperlanes, so if you're in a cantina near a spaceport on any major planet you're likely to hear Aqualish, Rodian and Durese. Learn a few phrases in each of these, plus Huttese. You don't want to waffle if someone says, "Hi chuba di naga?"

AT A GLANCE: UNUSUAL SYNTAX

Even if they speak Basic, be aware that some species, such as that of Jedi Master Yoda, rearrange subjects, verbs and objects in potentially confusing ways.

"Impossible to see the future is."

"Around the survivors a perimeter create!"

"The future is impossible to see."

"Create a perimeter around the survivors!"

Yoda, the last Jedi Grand Master

ANCIENT LANGUAGES
Some lost languages remain undecipherable. For example, even a protocol droid fluent in more than seven million forms of communication may struggle to translate ancient Jedi texts like the Aionomica and Rammahgon.

HOW TO COUNT TO 9 USING GALACTIC BASIC NUMERALS

0 =

1 = ⌐

2 = ☰

3 = Ⅎ

4 = Ⴑ

5 = ⊟

6 = ▱

7 = ⌐

8 = ⊟

9 = ▱

AUREBESH ALPHABET

Galactic Basic uses a 26-character alphabet, known as Aurebesh. It's the most widely used form of written language in the galaxy.

Aurek (a)	Besh (b)	Cresh (c)
Dorn (d)	Esk (e)	Forn (f)
Grek (g)	Herf (h)	Isk (i)
Jenth (j)	Krill (k)	Leth (l)
Mern (m)	Nern (n)	Osk (o)
Peth (p)	Qek (q)	Resh (r)
Senth (s)	Trill (t)	Usk (u)
Vev (v)	Wesk (w)	Xesh (x)
Yirt (y)	Zerek (z)	

HUTTESE: KEY PHRASES

"Pateesa." ·········· "Friend."

"Bargon wan che copa." ·········· "There will be no bargain."

"Coona tee-tocky malia?" ·········· "What took you so long?"

"Kuba, kayaba dee anko." · "Come to me."

"Boska!" ·········· "Let's go!"

"Hi chuba di naga?" ·········· "What do you want?"

SOCIAL MINEFIELDS

RELIGIONS OF THE GALAXY

IS THE FORCE JUST SIMPLE TRICKS AND NONSENSE? MAYBE... BUT IT HAS INSPIRED MOST GALACTIC FAITHS.

Time to get deep. The Force is an energy field generated by all life in the galaxy that binds everyone and everything, including inanimate objects. The Jedi and Sith are among its best-known adherents, but many other cultures also believe in the Force, even if they can't use it or sense it themselves.

THE JEDI ORDER
The Jedi are a monastic order dedicated to studying the Force's light side and using it for knowledge and peacekeeping.

⚠ WATCH OUT!

Sith Holocron

WHAT CREATES THE FORCE?
Midi-chlorians, microscopic life forms in the bloodstream of Force-sensitives, generate this energy field. But to match this "Living Force" is the "Cosmic Force" flowing across the galaxy from an inter-dimensional wellspring. That wellspring expressed itself to some as a physical place: Mortis.

THE SITH
The Sith embrace the dark side and the idea that you can impose your will on the Force and use it to control others.

THE DARK SIDE
Represented by the Son, the dark side is rage, fear and the desire for control.

The Mortis Force-wielders

THE BALANCE
The Father symbolised the equilibrium between dark and light.

THE LIGHT SIDE
The light side is peace. It was represented by the Daughter.

BEWARE!

Few Jedi or Sith remain, but Force devotees still exist, such as the dangerous Nightsisters of Dathomir, who access the Force through incantations and spells.

THE WHILLS

The Whills are a mysterious order who appear to use the Force to gain a cosmic perspective on galactic history. They believe in the Force even when they can't access it directly. This includes the Guardians – warriors who protect their traditions.

PILGRIMAGES

Because of the Force's cosmic aspect, some places are very strong with it. Such places can draw many different faiths, such as the Brotherhood of the Beatific Countenance.

AT A GLANCE: OTHER BELIEFS

Not all religions in the galaxy revolve around the Force. Other faiths involve very different beliefs and a wide range of rituals.

EWOKS

Ewoks worship forest spirits, though their shamans can quickly identify and revere new gods – and stage lavish feasts in their honour.

GUNGANS

Naboo's sentient amphibians, the Gungans, worship beings known as "the Guds". Beliefs include the "life debt" owed to whoever saves a Gungan's life.

MANDALORIANS

Historically, these warrior people worshiped war itself, with the armour they'd build being unique expressions of their identity.

79

DANGEROUS LOCALES

THESE ARE ESTABLISHMENTS WHERE THE COCKTAILS ARE SERVED COLD, BUT THE BLASTER FIRE IS ALWAYS HOT.

There are natural dangers throughout the galaxy, but none as dangerous as what sentient beings can devise – especially those driven into crime. For some reason, the scum and villainy of the galaxy's underbelly always seek each other out, and their favourite watering holes reek of peril.

AT HOME WITH THE SKYWALKERS
It isn't a specific locale, but associating with heroes can be just as bad for your health as associating with criminals. You may have your farm burnt or get frozen in carbonite.

Few windows (easier to hide nefarious activity)

Crumbling infrastructure is a safety hazard

TATOOINE: A WRETCHED HIVE
Like flies to dead meat, Tatooine's spaceport, Mos Eisley, has caused this backwater planet to attract beings of countless different species – many with dubious intentions.

MOS EISLEY CANTINA
Dimly lit, no frills bar run by the Wookiee Chalmun and grouchy bartender Wuher. Dismemberment? Allowed. Droids? Forbidden.

MOS ESPA GRAND ARENA
Open-air, bleacher-style seating for podraces: overcrowding, drunkenness, pickpockets, no guardrails and a Hutt in charge.

JABBA'S PALACE
Bounty hunters and smugglers abound upstairs, while a rancor lurks down below. If you decide to show up uninvited, pack thermal detonators.

BEWARE!

The Lodge is a bar and casino in the town of Fort Ypso, nestled high in the mountains of Vandor. Don't lose everything at the sabacc table or droid-fighting cage – you *really* don't want to get stuck here.

Cup of imitation juri juice

Stiff drinks to get drunk fast

Lengthy sleeves hide electronic cheating gear

An angry gambler who's lost winnings

THE WORST OF THE WORST

Some places are so dangerous that if you choose to visit them, an outside observer may assume you've given up on life. You may well lose it here, or simply vanish, never to be seen again.

CORUSCANT UNDERWORLD
WHY TO AVOID: With so many levels built on top of each other, it's unlikely emergency responders could ever find you.

MAZ'S CASTLE
WHY TO AVOID: It's neutral ground where mortal enemies are forced to play nice, and unwary patrons may get followed when they leave.

DATHOMIR
WHY TO AVOID: "Ain't nothing there but fog and witches", pirates are known to say. And sometimes reanimated corpses. Need we say more?

THE RING OF KAFRENE
WHY TO AVOID: It's a tangled nest of spies and stormtroopers, held together by gravitic bonds that could break any time.

ORGANISED CRIME

THEY WANT PROFIT, NOT EXCUSES. THOSE WHO DON'T PAY UP WILL BE PUNISHED, SO STEER WELL CLEAR.

Some trade in spice, others coaxium. Regardless of the racket, gangsters run their businesses with ruthless precision and a level of micromanagement even an Imperial loyalty officer might find too harsh. These crime bosses don't take "no" for an answer – always mind where you're standing in case one expresses their displeasure by activating a trapdoor.

⚠ WATCH OUT!

THE HUTT CARTEL
The five Hutt families control much of the galaxy's criminal activity from Nal Hutta and its seedy satellite, Nar Shaddaa – also known as the Smuggler's Moon.

GAPING MOUTH
Ziro spoke Basic with literate flair, though most Hutts speak only Huttese.

PRISON INK
A stint in Coruscant's maximum-security lock-up left Ziro with distinctive tattoos.

Ziro the Hutt, uncle of Jabba

STREET THIEVES
In places like Corellia, where poverty is rampant and work accidents have left behind orphans, petty crime lords like Lady Proxima train those without parents to steal on their behalf. Keep an eye on your credits!

HOW TO LEAVE A STREET GANG

1 Develop ace piloting skills by doing their bidding. Then pocket something valuable to pay your way and have a fast getaway vehicle fuelled up.

2 Bluff. Use a rock to pretend you have a thermal detonator – you'll have to mimic the clicking sound armed detonators make.

3 If your gang leader is a Grindalid, use your rock to smash a window, letting in sunlight to burn their skin – then put your piloting skills to the test!

CRIME BOSSES

Dryden Vos and other syndicate leaders develop brutal cults of personality. They throw parties, stage fancy floor shows, host podraces and then suddenly feed an attendee to a hungry beast or calmly murder an Imperial governor. Fear helps keep their subordinates in line.

Kyuzo petar blade

Striations of non-human origin

Dryden Vos

GANG WARS

The Hutts sometimes go to war with rival groups, hiring bounty hunters and mercenaries to carry out their bidding. Smaller groups such as Kanjikluh and the Guavian Death Gang are known to battle each other, too.

AT A GLANCE: GANGS OF THE GALAXY

Beyond the Hutts, there are many other criminal syndicates that conduct illicit business. Cross them at your peril.

CRIMSON DAWN
A secretive gang, publicly led by Dryden Vos and his lieutenant, Qi'ra, but ex-Sith Maul is really in charge.

PYKE SYNDICATE
Recognisable by their distinctively large skulls and small faces, the Pykes control Kessel's spice trade.

DESILIJIC CLAN
Arguably the most ruthless of the five Hutt families and the one that Jabba and Ziro both belonged to.

ZYGERRIAN SLAVERS

Zygerrians are feline bipeds with a taste for luxury, who run a slave trade across the Outer Rim. They find new slaves through kidnapping raids on remote worlds, such as Kiros and Jakku, and then sell them to criminal syndicates.

BLACK SUN
Ruled by the Falleen, known for their mind-altering pheromones, it's the most powerful non-Hutt gang.

GALACTIC GAMES AND HOW TO PLAY

SOME GAMES SO ARE SO COMMON IT WOULD BE EMBARRASSING IF YOU DIDN'T KNOW THE RULES. SO HERE THEY ARE.

There are few things more stressful than having to play a game you don't understand – especially if you're playing for money. Even if you don't gamble, you'll have to play sometimes to avoid becoming an outcast. There are almost as many games as there are stars in the sky, but some are so popular that you'll find them in every cantina from the Core to the Outer Rim.

DEJARIK
Two players move carved or holographic figurines of monsters around a board with three concentric circles.

AT A GLANCE: THE RULES OF DEJARIK

Each piece has a specific way of moving and attacking. If your piece lands on a spot occupied by an opponent, it kills it.

MONNOK
Sentient bipeds from Socorro who use crude spears against foes.

K'LOR'SLUG
Pink, tubular beast with a suction cup-like mouth and sharp teeth.

SCRIMP
Known only as Scrimp, this creature's origin has been lost to time.

MANTELLIAN SAVRIP
Grey, red-eyed sentient bruisers with powerful forearms.

GRIMTAASH THE MOLATOR
Mythical beast that once served Alderaanian royalty.

GHHHK
Insectoid species that is the apex predator in the fearsome jungles of Bith.

KINTAN STRIDER
Silicon-based life form from Kintan that can employ simple tools.

HOUJIX
Quadrupedal cephalopod capable of sending electric jolts through prey.

BULBOUS
Monster from Dorin that can emit toxic gasses to kill its enemies.

CORELLIAN SPIKE

A popular variant of the card game sabacc, corellian spike involves both chance and skill. There are 62 cards in the deck and all of them have a points value. The deck is made up of three suits, each of which contains 20 cards with values from -10 to +10. There are also two green sylop cards which have a value of zero. At the end of each round, the player whose hand has a value closest to zero wins (there are special rules if there's a tie). Players lose if they cannot bet any longer, and the game ends when a player wins with a value of zero.

WINNING THE GAME

There are many sabacc variants with a variety of hands. You must be incredibly lucky (or hideously unlucky) to get the hands shown below.

LOSING HAND
Not Nulrhek: three -10 cards and two -9 cards (a combined value of -48).

WINNING HAND
Pure sabacc: two green sylop cards (both of which have a value of zero).

DEIA'S DREAM

This is an Outer Rim game favoured by Culisetto, such as the Dengue Sisters. It involves a spinning board, easily turned by Culisetto snouts, and disk-shaped game tokens.

CHANCE CUBES

Chance cubes use gravity and randomisation to decide simple wagers. They can be used in pairs and other combinations, or feature as a part of other games.

⚠ WATCH OUT!

CHEATERS

Certain forms of sabacc use electronic decks and cheaters can wear concealed devices to change the value of their cards. Also, never roll a chance cube with a Jedi.

⚠ GAMBLING PERILS

IF YOU'RE A RISK TAKER, GAMBLING CAN HAVE GREAT REWARDS. BUT IT'S STILL A VERY, VERY BAD IDEA.

Our advice is simple: don't gamble. However, as we know you'll probably ignore that advice, we have also prepared some additional guidelines to prevent you from losing everything you own and/or being horribly killed. Read them very carefully, but remember: the house always wins.

HOW TO WIN A HAND OF SABACC

❶ The easiest way to win a hand of sabacc is to cheat. This is strongly recommended.

❷ If you have to play fair (again, not a sensible choice), closely watch your opponents for tells, to see if they are bluffing.

❸ Assess your cards carefully. Calculate the probabilities of your opponents' cards being better than yours, then play or fold accordingly.

GAMBLERS OF THE GALAXY
The best gamblers, i.e. the ones you really want to avoid playing against, can often be spotted quite easily.

WINNING STYLE
Ornate capes, expensive jewels and a confident swagger are all key warning signs.

HIDDEN ASSETS
A top-level gambler is also a big target. They will be heavily armed (and jumpy).

Lando Calrissian, gambler extraordinaire

⚠ WATCH OUT!

LOSING BIG
Do not bet more than you are willing to lose. If you bet your ship and get beaten, you're going to be stranded.

Gambling occurs across the galaxy, and gaming venues and their colourful clientele vary greatly. Choose wisely or the game might not be the only thing you lose.

CANTO BIGHT
High rollers only please! This gaudy, glitzy resort is where the galaxy's uber-wealthy gamble the fortunes of entire planets.

FORT YPSO LODGE
If you're after cosy surroundings, few laws and a mysterious background smell, Fort Ypso is the venue for you.

OUTLANDER CLUB
Gambling on Coruscant usually occurs in massive clubs like the Outlander. Be wary, as criminal gangs use them as a front.

LET THE WOOKIEE WIN
Not everyone takes losing gracefully. Some species react very badly, with gruesome results for the unprepared. Wookiees, especially, should be avoided as gaming partners due to their short tempers and penchant for limb removal. If in any doubt about the mood, strength or intentions of your gaming partner, subtly let them win and then escape the situation as fast as possible.

SOCIAL MINEFIELDS

ESSENTIAL GAMBLING EQUIPMENT
Some games are a matter of life and death, so take the time to prepare properly. A tool kit of essentials means you'll leave nothing – not even the game itself – to chance.

Cup for rolling chance cubes

Beverage cup (stay hydrated!)

Valuable dried chak-root

Selection of galactic coinage

Deck of sabacc cards

Chance cubes (ideally weighted)

"Honest stones" change colour in the presence of cheating technology

HIGH SOCIETY AND DRESS CODES

MAKING A SARTORIAL MISSTEP CAN BE LIKE FALLING INTO THE SARLACC PIT.

First impressions are everything, and let's face it, many beings in this galaxy are superficial. When mixing with the elite of the elite, making a fashion faux pas can be worse than getting into a firefight, so be prepared!

BLENDING IN

Sometimes you'll want to stand out from the crowd and shine as brightly as a supernova. But attention can attract danger. Dressing down to blend in can keep you safely anonymous. And if it so happens that everyone wants to stand out, you can have it both ways.

WHAT TO WEAR

1 An auropyle dress with matching headgear for when you're the centre of attention.

2 A parabolic headdress is good for concealing identity.

3 A long, unbroken silhouette is best if you have multiple eyes.

4 Dressing the colour of precious metals is always a popular choice.

5 Understated colours can give an air of refinement.

6 A monochromatic ensemble appeals to those who like military uniforms.

7 Cybernetic implants give a contemporary look.

8 Sometimes jewellery makes the strongest statement.

ELITE VENUES: GALAXIES OPERA HOUSE

Evening wear is a must, even if it's just to watch a repertory offering of a Mon Calamari opera classic and not a premiere. Seek out Baron Papanoida for scintillating conversation.

ELITE VENUES: CANTO BIGHT

Bring a shipful of Cantocoins to wager at the casino and don your most formal attire – don't look like you're someone who just crashed a shuttle on the beach.

LUXURY VEHICLES

If you have enough credits you'll never have to use public transit again. The rich prefer lushly appointed space yachts with the finest amenities.

FINE DINING

In the luxe life, you don't need to fill your stomach with every meal because more food is always available, so eat *slowly*. Rare ingredients and exotic tastes and textures are more important than packing in calories.

SURVIVING A NIGHT ON THE TOWN

THOSE WHO WORK HARD WANT TO PLAY HARD. BUT PLAYING HARD CAN BE DANGEROUS.

The twin suns have set on another day, but retiring to your bed or hibernation chamber is a long way off. Dressing up and heading to a nightclub, cantina or casino can be a perfect way to interact with clients in a more informal setting. Nightlife can lead to networking – but social hazards await.

CHOOSING A NIGHTCLUB
This is your most important decision. Maybe you like the latest Twi'lek dances, have a passion for the kloo horn or prefer to watch a podrace on a giant holographic display.

⚠ WATCH OUT!

MIXING DRINKS
At best, the wrong drink combination can be unfashionable. At worst, it can be fatal. Make sure you know your mixology or have a trustworthy bartender.

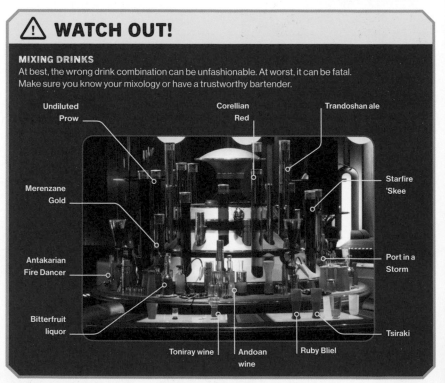

- Undiluted Prow
- Corellian Red
- Trandoshan ale
- Merenzane Gold
- Starfire 'Skee
- Antakarian Fire Dancer
- Port in a Storm
- Bitterfruit liquor
- Toniray wine
- Andoan wine
- Ruby Bliel
- Tsiraki

DRESSING FOR THE OCCASION

You don't want to be underdressed, nor do you want to be overdressed. Take some time to research the local fashions and pick out something that fits with your goals: perhaps you want to stand out and dazzle like a Naboo queen, or maybe you want a more understated look – a cloak and hood do wonders to cultivate an air of mystery. The best style reflects both who you are and what you want to become.

ASSESSING THE CROWD

Avoid any one-armed Aqualish or Wookiees playing dejarik. Mind your own business and keep to the edges of a club – that's usually where the most interesting beings can be found.

BITH CRANIUM
Biths' enlarged skulls allow them to perceive complex acoustics.

BEWARE!

Death Sticks are an illicit stimulant in the party scene of underworld Coruscant. Use will literally shorten you lifespan – hence the name. Try to avoid their lead purveyor, Elan "Sleazebaggano".

BANDS AND ENTERTAINMENT

No night is complete without music, but its quality can vary so choose wisely. Figrin D'an and the Modal Nodes are a safe bet. This popular band got stranded without funds on Tatooine. They have a long-running rivalry with Tatooine's other headliners, the Max Rebo Band.

Figrin D'an

SURVIVING ENCOUNTERS WITH FORCE USERS

"MAY THE FORCE STAY FAR AWAY FROM US" IS OUR MANTRA OF CHOICE.

Force users can be pretty terrifying. They can accomplish incredible acrobatic feats, battle entire armies single-handed and manipulate the thoughts and feelings of others. The best survival strategy is to avoid them altogether.

JEDI POWERS

Using their knowledge of the Force for peacekeeping, wisdom and defence, the Jedi are likely the most benevolent Force users you could encounter – so unless you have the death sentence on 12 systems you'll probably be fine.

SPIRIT
WHAT IS IT: No, that's not a bluish-green hologram you're seeing, it's a Jedi who's become "one with the Force" instead of dying. Very few Jedi have mastered this skill.

JEDI MIND TRICK
WHAT IS IT: Are you already open to the power of suggestion? Oh, weak-minded one, you'll stand no chance. Jedi can make you do things with a wave of their hands.

TELEKINESIS
WHAT IS IT: Jedi can lift incredible weights or summon objects, such as their lightsaber, with just the power of their minds. If things start flying around, watch out.

LEAP
WHAT IS IT: They're not secretly wearing rocket boots. Jedi can hurl themselves up to astonishing heights. That lofty alcove you're hiding in won't put you out of reach.

AT A GLANCE: LIGHTSABERS

Surely the most dangerous personal weapon ever devised, lightsabers can cut through virtually anything. Unless you have the power of the Force to wield one properly, you are practically asking to sever one of your own limbs.

SITH POWERS

Unlike the Jedi, the Sith are actively looking for trouble. They feed off their victims' fear and anger and lead lives fuelled by hate, so their powers are far more unnatural than those of the Jedi. If faced with a Sith, you are dealing with an almost unstoppable killing machine. Good luck!

TELEKINESIS
WHAT IS IT: Sith won't just move things with their minds, they will turn ordinary objects into ballistic weapons to hurl at you. Or simply hurl you into the ceiling yourself.

FRENZY
WHAT IS IT: Sith draw deeply on the dark side of the Force to get into a berserker rage. Try not to make them angry – though they probably already are.

LIGHTNING
WHAT IS IT: Shooting lightning from their fingers is a Sith speciality. There's no defence unless you're carrying a lightsaber to deflect it, but that has its own risks (see above).

CHOKE
WHAT IS IT: If you suddenly feel your trachea (or xenobiological equivalent) mysteriously closing, a Sith is strangling you from afar. Don't play dead – it won't work!

HOW TO AVOID OFFENDING A HUTT

HUTTS BARELY NEED AN EXCUSE TO FEED YOU TO A VARIETY OF GIANT BEASTS – DON'T GIVE THEM ONE.

With a Hutt as your friend you'll enjoy fancy floor shows and spice. With a Hutt as your enemy you'll find yourself plunging through a trapdoor into a rancor's den, with the crime lord's guests wagering over what part of you gets eaten first. The former is preferable, though that means you're probably involved in criminal activity and should rethink your life choices.

SAVOURY DELICACIES
Nothing creates a welcoming atmosphere like meat roasting on a spit.

ELEVATED DAIS
Jabba positions himself in the best vantage point to see and be seen.

BEWARE!

Guests who seek an audience with Jabba must look up to speak with the Hutt. Directing their gaze upwards means they're often unaware of how precarious a footing they have below.

TRAPDOOR
The unsuspecting damned will find the floor falling open beneath them.

HUTT HOSPITALITY: DO OR DO NOT...

DO... bring gifts to honour his or her exaltedness. Hutts goes through interpreters at a high rate, so a new protocol droid is never a bad idea. Astromechs can be handy for serving drinks to the Hutt's guests.

DO NOT... mess with their wall art. It might not look like Hutts care about interior decorating, but they do, especially if their aesthetic involves carbonite.

DO... show a little backbone. Wasting their Rodian bounty hunter or threatening to blow up their palace with a thermal detonator might actually earn you their respect.

DO NOT... avoid paying a Hutt. Evor. Not even if a meteorite destroys your spice mine. Not even if Imperials board your ship. Always *always* pay the Hutt.

DO... shut up and play the hits if you're there to perform. Your Hutt patron may want you to repeat a song or have a dancer perform twice. Comply.

DO NOT... assume a Hutt is sleeping. Sometimes they just want to catch you in the act of whatever underhanded trickery you're engaged in.

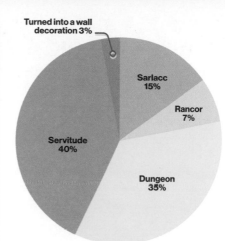

Turned into a wall decoration 3%

Sarlacc 15%

Rancor 7%

Servitude 40%

Dungeon 35%

JABBA'S PUNISHMENTS

Punishment serves dual purposes for Jabba: enforcement and entertainment. Making a harsh example of someone means others will be less likely to cross him. And it's fun for everybody else.

ESCAPE,
EVASION AND
INFILTRATION

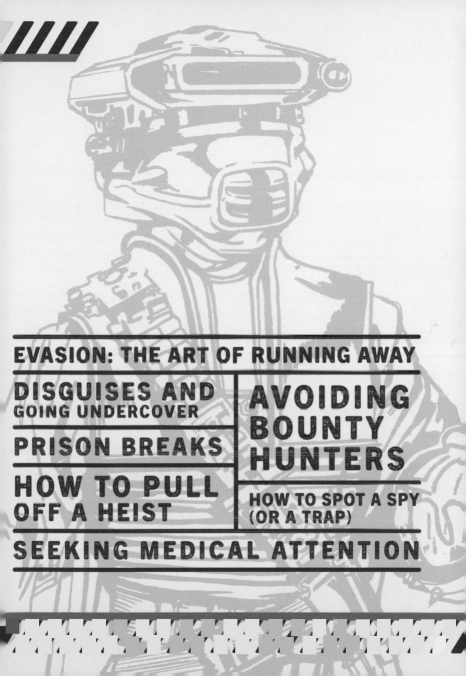

EVASION: THE ART OF RUNNING AWAY

LIVING TO FIGHT ANOTHER DAY ALWAYS BEATS DYING IN A DRAMATIC FASHION.

There is no shame in running. Keeping your hide is always more important than keeping your honour – but generally you can keep both if you make a truly artful exit. You'll need to think fast on your feet with pursuers on your tail, though. Hopefully, you're handy with a blaster, have a getaway vehicle ready and have an astromech able to spray smoke to conceal your escape.

TIPS FOR HIDING
The most important thing is simply to stay quiet. Have your blaster drawn in case you get spotted, but keep ducked in the shadows or behind a corner or obstacle – let your surroundings shield you.

⚠ WATCH OUT!

VEHICLE CHASES
Lean into your skill set – if you know you can handle hairpin turns and navigate at high speeds through many obstacles, consider flying into an asteroid field. There's a good chance your pursuers won't be able to dodge the asteroids the way you can.

M-68 landspeeder

GETAWAY VEHICLES
Your best bet is something with fast acceleration, a sleek profile that's hard to hit and can squeeze through tight spaces, and has powerful thrusters to make sharp turns.

HOW TO BLEND INTO A CROWD

1 Do some initial research on the crowd in question before you even get there: what do they wear, what would they be talking about?

2 Having researched potential small-talk, do converse with members of the crowd. Keeping silent and to yourself breeds suspicion.

3 When you're trying to look inconspicuous, one of the trickiest questions can be what to do with your hands. It's a good idea to hold something, like a drink.

4 Don't keep near the centre of the crowd, but don't linger near the edge either – and look like you're having a good time! Nothing stands out like a party pooper.

EVADING PURSUERS: DO OR DO NOT...

DO... contact your allies to ask for help. Send messages on a secure, encrypted channel or your pursuers might trace your transmission to them.

DO NOT... leave your comrades without having first designated a rendezvous spot. And establish times to check-in with allies so they'll know something's wrong if there's no response.

DO... use deception, if speed won't save you. Imperial Star Destroyers are so big they'd never even know you've attached to their hull to hide out.

DO NOT... forget to look behind you if you decide to conceal your ship among a Star Destroyer's ejected garbage. A bounty hunter may have had the same idea.

LAST RESORTS
Sometimes your only way out may be to take a leap of faith. If you're cornered on a narrow ledge extending over an abyss and capture seems inevitable, it's worth considering the other option. You may fall to your death, but if you're lucky, industrial air jets may catch you and direct you to the safety of an air shaft.

SELF SACRIFICE
Sometimes escape just isn't possible. In this situation, consider helping friends or family to flee by distracting your pursuers.

HOW TO RETREAT
It's easier to run when it's just you and a few friends. If you have an entire military base to evacuate it's going to be more complicated. A "Kay-One-Zero" retreat order will send your ground troops to secure your perimeter and your flyers into the air to attack the approaching enemy assault. This defensive counter-attack is essential for buying non-combat personnel time to secure vital cargo. They should be able to escape while you give protective cover.

BEWARE!
If you have to make a hasty exit, pack essentials, pack lightly and keep the mementos to a minimum. Take the rations, leave the cuddly tooka doll.

DISGUISES AND GOING UNDERCOVER

THERE ARE TIMES WHEN STAYING ALIVE MEANS PRETENDING TO BE SOMEONE ELSE.

Learning to disguise yourself is a vital survival skill, so learn it well. Maybe you need to sneak into a dangerous location or maybe you've made some lethal enemies? Either way, the sad reality is that at some point, someone, somewhere is going to try to disintegrate you. The best way to avoid that is by not looking like you.

IMPROVISATION
When there's no time for elaborate disguises you may have to improvise. As BB-8 discovered, a trash can is a great way to conceal a droid.

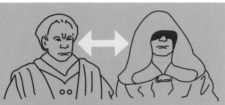

HIDING IN PLAIN SIGHT
Remember that Force users can manipulate the thoughts and feelings of those around them. This allows them to hide their true natures, so be vigilant!

DISGUISED DECOY
If, like Queen Amidala of Naboo, you are worried that somebody might be after you, a decoy is very useful. In the event that your suspicions are correct, it's the decoy who will take the hit, not you. For this reason, try to find a decoy that you are not emotionally attached to.

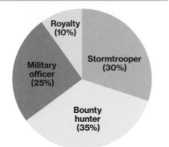

Pie chart:
- Royalty (10%)
- Stormtrooper (30%)
- Military officer (25%)
- Bounty hunter (35%)

MOST COMMON DISGUISES
Imperial uniforms make the best disguises, but bounty hunter outfits are also a popular choice.

IMPERIAL INFILTRATION

Many military personnel have uniforms that cover their faces. Rogue One took advantage of this fact when they had to sneak into an Imperial base – you should do the same

INFILTRATION: DO OR DO NOT...

DO... your homework! Find out as much as you can about the situation you are going into. Learn passwords and secret codes in advance.

DO NOT... draw attention to yourself. Try to blend into the background. Be boring, unremarkable and highly forgettable. Try to avoid interacting with others, but...

DO... speak if spoken to. Nothing is more suspicious than an awkward silence. Try to sound like you know what you're talking about.

DO NOT... panic! Even with all of the advice on these pages, it is highly likely that you will be discovered. Be ready for when that happens and have a plan for a quick escape.

LOCAL CLOTHING
People across the galaxy are naturally suspicious of outsiders. Go local to help blend in.

MASKS
Wearing a disguise that conceals your face and alters your voice at the same time is a great idea.

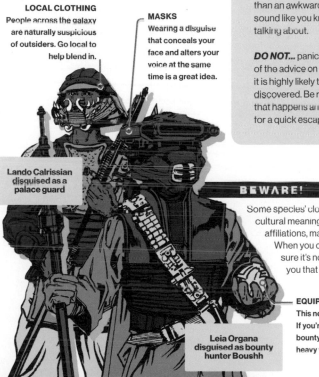

Lando Calrissian disguised as a palace guard

Leia Organa disguised as bounty hunter Boushh

BEWARE!

Some species' clothing can have hidden cultural meanings, such as clan affiliations, marital status or gender. When you choose a disguise, make sure it's not saying things about you that you did not intend!

EQUIPMENT
This needs to be appropriate: If you're impersonating a bounty hunter, you'll need the heavy weapons to match.

PRISON BREAKS

IF YOU ARE IMPRISONED UNJUSTLY OR ARE A PRISONER OF WAR, IT'S YOUR DUTY TO TRY TO BREAK OUT.

In a galaxy at war, many wrong assumptions can be made and incorrect conclusions drawn, and even if you're not actively working for any particular side in the conflict, combatants may prefer to just lock you up and ask questions later. Escape should become your one and only mission.

PRISONERS OF WAR

The Empire has Accresker Jail, made of gravitically bonded wreckage towed through space, and the rebels have Sunspot Prison, hiding in the corona of a star. The Empire often executes rebel prisoners, so escape as soon as you can.

BEWARE!

Even if their layouts are similar, each prison is unique and will have its own weaknesses. But one thing is true for all of these – you will need help from outside to break out.

WOBANI LABOUR CAMP

A muddy industrial world for Imperial prisoners sentenced to hard labour – a full assault team will be required to escape.

CANTO BIGHT POLICE HEADQUARTERS

City jails are usually less secure. A little slicing skill and a helpful astromech should spell freedom.

REPUBLIC CENTRAL DETENTION CENTRE

Cells at this facility can only be accessed by repulsorcraft – hire a bounty hunter to aid you.

DETENTION BLOCKS

Imperial prisons, whether on planets, ships or space stations, have the same standard layout: a central security hub with cell-lined corridors that radiate out like spokes, all secured by cameras and automated guns.

LIFE IN PRISON

It's a grind. For one, you never know who your cellmate will be. It could be someone who will help you escape or someone who says they're going to kill you each day. Except for sensitive political prisoners, the Empire likes to

use prisoners for hard labour – this can actually be a good thing, as prisoner transports can be vulnerable to hijacking and escape attempts.

HOW TO RESCUE A PRINCESS

1 Steal stormtrooper armour and have your Wookiee co-pilot pose as your prisoner.

2 Tell the Wookiee to go wild as soon as you're in the detention block, creating the distraction you need. While they try to restrain the Wookiee, neutralise the guards.

3 Take out all the wall-mounted auto-targeting blasters. Use the control console to find the princess' cell.

4 Take the princess' crack about your height in your stride and give her a blaster – her shooting skills will be needed.

5 Listen to her when she says to jump into the garbage chute.

Just as your environment will shape your escape strategy, so too should your skill set.

CAUSE A RIOT
WHAT TO DO: Fellow prisoners always want to escape too. Enlist their aid – a group can be an overpowering force.

PICK THE LOCK
WHAT TO DO: Work on your slicing skills so you can hack into any lock mechanism. Also, learn to bend your arm in weird ways.

USE THE FORCE
WHAT TO DO: If you're lucky enough to be Force-sensitive, using a Jedi Mind Trick on your guard is the way to go.

BREAKING IN
The only thing riskier than breaking out of prison is breaking into prison. Sometimes this is necessary to get someone out. Make certain you have a plan if you're caught – your jailer may decide prison is too good for you and simply try to execute you instead.

ESCAPE, EVASION AND INFILTRATION

103

HOW TO PULL OFF A HEIST

WE CAN'T SAY THAT THIS GUIDE TO GALACTIC HAZARDS IS MEANT FOR CRIMINALS. BUT WE CAN'T SAY IT ISN'T EITHER.

Not that you would ever attempt such blatant criminality, but perhaps you intend some galactic tourism to the spots in question? These heists are certainly legendary, involving figures with a penchant for self-mythologizing. Here's what we think really happened. And if someone should try to copy these thieves, we bear no responsibility for the matter.

AT A GLANCE: VANDOR CONVEYEX

The frigid, mountainous world of Vandor has a crisscrossing network of hover trains – the conveyex – that transport precious cargo. Beckett's gang tried to lift one.

1

RECONNAISSANCE
First, Beckett's gang scouted the route, velocity and timing of a conveyex bearing a haul of coaxium.
OUTCOME: Success

2

INFILTRATION
Flying a craft with strong repulsorlifts, they were able to hover in the conveyex's blindspot and drop off a team.
OUTCOME: Success

3

THE STEAL
Hot-wiring and slicing skills were needed to get inside and lift the valuable coaxium.
OUTCOME: Success

4

EXTRACTION
This is where it went wrong. A rival gang, Enfys Nest's Cloud-Riders, arrived too, blowing the Beckett gang's cover. The fight over the payload caused it to be jettisoned and destroyed.
OUTCOME: Failure

HEIST FAILED

⊗

AT A GLANCE: KESSEL VAULT

In the Vandor raid it was possible the targets wouldn't even detect the raiders.
The Kessel heist, however, required theatrical deception and role-playing.

1

RECONNAISSANCE
Beckett's gang got intel from Crimson
Dawn, a syndicate supposedly friendly
with the Pykes who control Kessel. This
info allowed a daring plan to be hatched.
OUTCOME: Success

2

INFILTRATION
Qi'ra of Crimson Dawn joined the mission
and went undercover as a slaver so she
would be let in by the Pykes — she brought
a Wookiee "slave" as a welcome gift.
OUTCOME: Success

3

THE STEAL
The Wookiee broke free and the gang's
droid, L3-37, staged a droid revolt as
a distraction. As panic engulfed the
Pykes, the gang stole the coaxium.
OUTCOME: Success

4

EXTRACTION
The gang had a getaway ship capable
of evading the many hazards around
the planet, such as the Maw black hole,
and made the Kessel Run in 12 parsecs.
OUTCOME: Success

**HEIST
SUCCESSFUL**

PROFIT?
A heist can lead to great
wealth – and losing
everything else. But better
to be lonely and rich, than
lonely and poor, right?

ESCAPE, EVASION AND INFILTRATION

105

AVOIDING BOUNTY HUNTERS

IT SHOULD BE SIMPLE: DON'T DO ANYTHING THAT GETS A BOUNTY PLACED ON YOUR HEAD!

Owe money to a Hutt? Rebelling against our glorious Emperor? Have the death sentence on 12 systems? There are few reasons why a bounty hunter should be after you, none of them good. Maybe try paying your debts and abiding by the law. In the event of poor life choices or an extreme case of mistaken identity, though, here's what you should do. Luckily, bounty hunters are quite easy to spot.

WHAT TO LOOK OUT FOR

Most bounty hunters are imposing but not flashy. If someone looks like they're carrying their own mini-arsenal, especially of unusual weapons like flamethrowers, and have a general aura of hostility, they may be a bounty hunter. Especially if they're in a cantina, which are their go-to networking spots.

BOUNTY HUNTERS: DO OR DO NOT...

DO... shoot first and ask questions later. There's no such thing as unfair when dealing with bounty hunters. They know what business they're in.

DO NOT... stop looking behind you if you suspect you're being followed. Complacency will just get you frozen in carbonite.

DO... offer them a better price than the being who hired them, if you have deep pockets. Credits can corrupt any bounty hunter.

DO NOT... make it personal. It's bad if they're after you for money, worse if they hate your guts (or intestinal equivalent).

BATTERED ARMOUR
If it's scuffed and dented, it means they've been through a lot but are still standing.

CAPE
Seems inadvisable for one who wields a flamethrower, but good for concealment.

Boba Fett, bounty hunter

⚠ WATCH OUT!

KEY BOUNTY HUNTERS

No two bounty hunters are alike. They all have different skill sets and their weaponry can vary widely. A counterattack you've prepared against one may be useless against another.

If hunted by **Dengar**: Pull off bandages, even if they're a style choice more than a medical necessity.

If hunted by **Aurra Sing**: Aim for antenna in skull – supposedly it senses enemies' fear.

If hunted by **Embo**: Steal hat he uses as a weapon and sled. Beware his anooba.

If hunted by **IG-88**: Find droid poppers (Clone Wars-era anti-droid weapons), to short his circuits.

If hunted by **Bossk**: Lure him with scent of Wookiee to a refrigerated room (he's cold-blooded).

If hunted by **4-LOM**: Probably not working alone. Keep an eye out for this droid's partner, Zuckuss.

HOW TO SPOT A SPY (OR A TRAP)

IF SOMEONE OR SOMETHING SEEMS TOO GOOD TO BE TRUE, THEY PROBABLY ARE.

A false sense of security is your biggest enemy. That attractive cantina patron sidling up to you at the bar may not have your best interests at heart, and that shadowy figure minding their own business might actually be minding yours. Remain vigilant: the last thing you want is to end up in a situation where you have to yell, "It's a trap!"

GARINDAN
Don't call him "Long-Snoot". This Kubaz with the prominent proboscis, hooded cloak and squeaky voice is one of Mos Eisley's sneakiest informants. Mind what you're doing while in town – you never know where he'll be.

⚠ WATCH OUT!

SPOTTING A SPY
Eyes darting back and forth, an elbow slightly bent for easy holster access, an air of trying a little too hard to be inconspicuous – these are all key warning signs. There's a very good chance this being may have a secret agenda.

SPY GEAR
Forged travel documents and data-slicing equipment.

STRIKING GOOD LOOKS
Weaponised handsomeness to lure the unsuspecting.

PISTOL
Concealable sidearm for dealing with "problems".

COVER BLOWN
A cornered spy is a dangerous and unpredictable one – if they're caught while on a cloak-and-dagger mission, they won't hesitate to use the dagger.

Cassian Andor, rebel spy

WHAT ARE BOTHANS?

Some say Bothans are specialists at skulduggery. They were instrumental in retrieving key intelligence about the second Death Star, though their mortality rate on that quest was extremely high.

ESCAPING ASSASSINATION

Whether secretly planting bombs on your landing platform or sliding insect-like kouhuns into your boudoir, assassins can be hard to shake. Consider hiring a body double if you have the credits (see page 100).

⚠ AT A GLANCE: IS IT A TRAP?

Not all traps are as easy to spot as a gundark nest, but these infamous ones all had warning signs that trouble lay ahead.

ORDER 66
WARNING SIGN: Your clone trooper escort speaking to a mysterious hooded hologram, saying "It will be done, my lord".

BECKETT'S SHOWDOWN
WARNING SIGN: Beckett prattling on about retiring to Glee Anselm while his hand slides slowly towards his holster.

LANDO'S HOSPITALITY
WARNING SIGN: Your host flirting a bit too aggressively, plus the sudden unexplained destruction of your droid.

REBEL FLEET AT ENDOR
WARNING SIGN: The enemy jamming your sensors when they supposedly don't know that you're coming.

THE FINE ART OF DOUBLE CROSSING

The best way to pull off a double-cross is also the riskiest: make your mark think you're betraying them – say, that the coaxium you've given them is fake – so they end up prematurely showing their hand. This approach will inevitably require decent combat skills.

⚠ SEEKING MEDICAL ATTENTION

DON'T LET YOUR PRIDE GET BETWEEN YOU AND A MED DROID IF YOU'RE MISSING AN ARM.

Galactic medicine has had thousands of years of evolution, and there's a solution for practically every ailment that presents itself as long as the patient has the will to live. While death itself still cannot be cheated, at least these treatments can help keep it at bay. Depending on your access to medical attention, an otherwise fatal injury can be just a minor inconvenience.

PROSTHETIC LIMBS

Losing a limb is a frequent occurrence in a galaxy of lightsabers and volcano-set combat. Prostheses connect to nerve endings to replicate fully the operation and feeling of the missing limb. You can opt for a synth-flesh covered version to match your skin or scale-tone or embrace a more functional, metallic look.

⚠ AT A GLANCE: MED LABS

The most important component of a med lab is the bacta tank. Bacta is a unique liquid that promotes rapid healing of wounds. Tanks of it allow for total immersion of the critically wounded.

2-1B
medical droid

MEDICAL EQUIPMENT

A flesh-and-blood doctor with a medical degree from an accredited galactic university or a med droid with the equivalent software should know how to use any of these basic med-lab tools.

REPULSOR GURNEY

The repulsorlift provides a cushion of air to smoothly transport a patient in maximum comfort.

MED KIT

A med kit comes stocked with many different tools to promote recovery, including bacta patches to apply to smaller wounds.

SURGICAL DROID

These droids are programmed to perform all surgical procedures. They can stitch up wounds with computerised precision.

MEDICAL FRIGATES

These lightly armed ships have many airlocks to facilitate the rapid transfer of patients from multiple other ships at once. The Nebulon-B frigate is commonly used as a hospital ship because its modular interior is easily modified from warship functions to surgical suites and med labs.

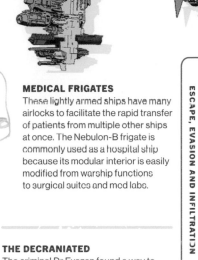

THE DECRANIATED

The criminal Dr Evazan found a way to have sentient beings survive even after removing their brains, allowing them to be controlled. Some still seem to have minds of their own, though.

MEDICAL HORRORS

Even the most horrific scenarios can still have happy endings depending on how you look at it. Even one who has lost all of their limbs and suffered horrific burns by getting far too close to a lava flow can survive by spending the rest of their lives inside a medically calibrated suit of armour. You'll have to get used to the heavy breathing.

EXPOSED INTESTINES

Neurological signals are muted for the decraniated.

111

DANGEROUS CREATURES

DEADLY PREDATORS

THE SARLACC

WATER MONSTERS

WHEN A CAVE *ISN'T* A CAVE: ENCOUNTERS WITH MEGAFAUNA

WHAT TO DO IF YOU'VE BEEN EATEN

PARASITES AND POISONOUS CREATURES

DEADLY PREDATORS

THE GALAXY IS FULL OF CREATURES THAT WANT TO KILL AND EAT YOU. HERE'S HOW TO AVOID BEING LUNCH.

There are things in the galaxy that not even your worst nightmares could create. Claws, fangs and tentacles combine into all kinds of horrific shapes, and all of them think you look delicious. The best guidance of all is: do not go where these things live. If that doesn't work, here are a few pointers that might give you a fighting chance.

⚠ WATCH OUT!

WAMPAS
Wampas are dangerous ambush predators. They are often more than 3 m (9 ft 10 in) tall and can weigh in excess of 150 kgs (330 lbs).

THICK FUR
This keeps out the cold and also gives the wampa added resistance to weapons. Aim for the face!

DEADLY CLAWS
Designed to rip through thick tauntaun hides, these claws will definitely leave a mark.

TEETH
These razor-sharp fangs can strip flesh from bone with a single bite.

HOW TO SURVIVE A WAMPA ATTACK

1 If you are hanging from the ceiling like Luke Skywalker, proceed to Step 2. If you're not, that's great! Head straight to Step 3.

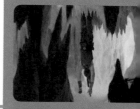

2 Find a way to detach yourself from the ice. A lightsaber works best; failing that, use a blaster, but don't shoot yourself in the foot.

3 You're going to have a very angry wampa after you. Hit, blast or slice it with whatever you have available, then get out of there fast!

AT A GLANCE: PREDATORS

Make sure you know one type of big toothy creature from another and what to do if one is after you.

ACKLAY
WHAT TO DO: Don't bother running – you'll just die tired. If you have a lightsaber, go for the legs, but watch out for the razor-sharp front limbs!

NEXU
WHAT TO DO: Pretty much your only option is to put yourself out of reach. Climb as high as you can and stay there.

RANCOR
WHAT TO DO: Once a rancor gets its claws around you, it'll try to bite off your head. Keep moving to make yourself a harder target.

RATHTAR
WHAT TO DO: I'm not going to lie, you're in real trouble here. Hiding might be your best bet, as rathtars are largely blind.

CORELLIAN HOUND
WHAT TO DO: Cover yourself in something smelly – like fish guts – to avoid the hounds' finely attuned sense of smell.

REEK
WHAT TO DO: Reeks are strong but not particularly nimble. Wait for it to charge, then dodge to the side to avoid getting the horn.

⚠ THE SARLACC

"IN HIS BELLY YOU WILL FIND A NEW DEFINITION OF PAIN AND SUFFERING..."

Is it an animal or is it a plant? Scientists don't know for certain because they're simply unwilling to get too close. Related to the rathtars and the blixus, Sarlaccs burrow underground up to 100 metres (328 feet) when they reach maturity and digest anything that falls into their gaping maws.

Tentacles grasp any prey that wanders too close

FEEDING TIME
Tatooine's Great Pit of Carkoon housed an ancient, giant Sarlacc. Jabba the Hutt would stage ritual executions by feeding the condemned to the beast.

SARLACCS: DO OR DO NOT...

DO... fire a blaster at a tentacle if it grabs you – you'll be released.

DO NOT... wander near the edge of a Sarlacc pit. What are you doing there at all? Don't mess around!

DO... wear armour so you'll take longer to digest. This may give you an opportunity to escape.

DO NOT... offend a Hutt so much that he or she feels compelled to feed you to one.

GETTING EATEN

Of all the horrible fates in the galaxy, this is possibly the very worst. A Sarlacc uses neurotoxins to paralyse its victims and then keeps them in constant agony while they're devoured. By placing them into a hibernation state, the Sarlacc ensures they remain alive for all 1,000 years of digestion.

Spiny teeth prevent victims from escaping

Beak-like tongue leads to multiple stomachs

BEWARE!

If you're wearing armour and have enough weapons, you may be able to blast your way out even after you've been eaten. But beware of fellow victims in the gullet – they may be desperate and dangerous.

WATER MONSTERS

MAKING SURE THERE'S ENOUGH OXYGEN IN YOUR TANKS ISN'T YOUR ONLY CONCERN WHEN HEADING BENEATH THE WAVES.

Watery depths conceal much. On planets that have vast oceans, such as the subterranean seas of Naboo, briny beasts can lurk – some of them incredibly massive. But though their bodies are large, their brains are often small: for some reason they think metallic underwater craft look tasty. Hopefully yours has a strong hull. You're going to need it.

⚠ WATCH OUT!

SANDO AQUA MONSTER
The apex predator in the seas of Naboo, this skyscraper-sized leviathan is one of the largest aquatic life forms found anywhere in the galaxy.

TAIL
Provides main propulsion, can also function as a grasping limb.

SIZE CHART

Sando aqua monster
160 m (525 ft)

→
Gungan bongo submarine
15 m (49 ft)

MAW
Jaws large enough to envelop any underwater creature.

HOW TO AVOID A SANDO AQUA MONSTER

1 They live only in the deepest part of Naboo's underground seas – what are you doing there? Fleeing from one or distracting it are the only ways to escape.

2 Make certain you're travelling in a Gungan-rated bongo. It might just be speedy enough to avoid flying into the beast's gaping maw. Your only other hope is to lure it to an even tastier meal.

3 Steer your bongo in the direction of an opee sea killer or colo claw fish. The sando aqua monster will sate itself with one of those over cold metal.

BEWARE!

These beasts may not be as gargantuan as the sando aqua monster, but they are just as hungry and just as deadly.

COLO CLAW FISH

The only way to escape is to lure it into a sando aqua monster's mouth. Some people say its meat is delicious, though, so who's the real predator?

BLIXUS

The Sarlacc is immobile, the rathtar can roll itself with its tentacles and this, their aquatic cousin, is a fast swimmer. Hack at its tentacles with a vibroaxe.

KWAZEL MAW

An amphibious predator native to Rodia. If you're feeling brave, try taming this beast – it can become a useful steed.

GOING UNDERWATER: DO OR DO NOT...

DO... make certain you have ample reserves of fuel and oxygen in your sub when preparing for an extended undersea trip. Desperately gasping for air is never a good look.

DO NOT... travel with a Gungan who has a proven history of crashing submersible craft and a personality prone to panic.

DO... equip your bongo with an electrification system to send a few thousand volts through any beast that wraps its jaws around your hull.

DO NOT... panic. Keeping a cool head is essential if you're to avoid becoming a meal. Remember: there's always a bigger fish.

DANGEROUS CREATURES

AT A GLANCE: OPEE SEA KILLER

A hard, shell-like skin protects the opee sea killer, while its tongue can grasp hold of anything.

"DIO GOOBERFISH!"

The opee sea killer is fast and difficult to shake off. Its tongue can attach itself to prey with the strength of a vacuum seal and then pull the prey directly back into its waiting jaws.

Antenna provides sonar navigation

Suction-cup tongue

WHEN A CAVE *ISN'T* A CAVE: ENCOUNTERS WITH MEGAFAUNA

SOME BEASTS ARE SO MASSIVE YOU MIGHT NOT EVEN REALISE THEY'RE BEASTS.

The galaxy is full of wonders to boggle the imagination and dangers more lethal than you could ever imagine. Some creatures are so large they can be mistaken for asteroids or other inanimate objects. Generally, these giant life forms won't bother you unless you bother them, but it pays to be prepared.

LARGEST MEGAFAUNA
These life forms are so huge they can live only in the most remote environments.

Length (metres)

Exogorth	Zillo Beast	Summa-verminoth	Joopa
900 m (2,953 ft)	97 m (318 ft)	7,432 m (24,383 ft)	21 m (69 ft)

⚠ WATCH OUT!

ZILLO BEAST

These massive creatures once roamed Malastare. They were believed extinct until a Republic bomb roused one from the depths of the planet. Their scales are so strong they can deflect a lightsaber blade. You likely won't run into one, but if you do you can neutralise it with a concentrated application of Malastarian fuel.

TAIL SPIKES
Can smash starfighters out of the air with a whip-like motion.

SIZE CHART

Republic gunship
17.4 m
(57 ft)

Zillo Beast
97 m
(318 ft)

The gigantic summa-verminoths dwell in the Akkadese Maelstrom

HOW TO ESCAPE A SUMMA-VERMINOTH

1 Engage in evasive manoeuvres – summa-verminoths have many eyes, but flying rapidly through its tentacles will distract it.

2 Lure it close to a black hole. If it gets too close to the singularity, its extremely large mass should cause it to get sucked in.

3 Make sure you lure it to the singularity without getting sucked in yourself – the fastest of ships will be needed.

BEWARE!

You might not immediately realise the mist you're surrounded by is in fact the intestinal gases of an exogorth – as the crew of the *Millennium Falcon* discovered when they barely escaped.

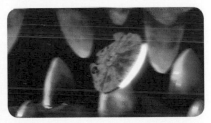

JOOPA

Joopas are giant worm-like creatures that lurk below the silicate surface of Seelos. They can be defeated with laser-cannon blasts – but you'll have to lure one to a place where you can get a proper firing solution, and for that you'll need bait. A Lasat crewmate should do nicely

EXOGORTH (SPACE SLUG)

These silicon-based life forms can survive in a vacuum, but usually like to live inside asteroids for protection, waiting to emerge and snatch passing prey with their huge maws. Their massive internal cavities can replicate an atmosphere, though it's not breathable by humans.

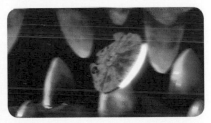

WHAT TO DO IF YOU'VE BEEN EATEN

IF YOU HAVE FOLLOWED THE ADVICE IN THIS CHAPTER, THIS SHOULD NOT HAPPEN. BUT JUST IN CASE IT DOES...

First of all, don't panic. It might feel like game over, but with a bit of luck and ingenuity, you might just make it out alive. As a rule, big creatures have slow digestive systems, so you should at least have some time to play with. Just follow this step-by-step guide.

START

ARE YOU STILL IN ONE PIECE?

ARE YOU BEING RAPIDLY DISSOLVED?

You are dead!

DO YOU STILL HAVE YOUR LEGS?

CAN YOU STILL MOVE?

CAN YOU CLIMB TOWARDS IT?

You are dead!

You are dead!

CAN YOU SEE A LIGHT ANYWHERE?

DO YOU HAVE ANY TOOLS WITH YOU?

ARE THEY WILLING TO JOIN FORCES?

DO YOU HAVE ANYONE ELSE WITH YOU?

You are dead!

ARE YOU WILLING TO GET... GOOEY?

You are dead!

DO EITHER OF YOU HAVE ANY ESCAPE EQUIPMENT?

You are dead!

CAN YOU ESCAPE OUT THE "BACK END?"

IS YOUR ESCAPE EQUIPMENT EFFECTIVE?

IS THERE ANYTHING BLOCKING THE EXIT?

You are dead!

You are dead!

CAN YOU CUT YOUR WAY OUT?

You are dead!

CONGRATULATIONS!

You've made it out. That wasn't so hard, was it?
Let this be a lesson to avoid large, dangerous,
hungry monsters in future.

PARASITES AND POISONOUS CREATURES

THEY'LL SNEAK UP ON YOU AND POISON YOU – OR WORSE, PUT YOU UNDER THEIR CONTROL – WHEN YOU LEAST EXPECT IT.

Luckily, all of these creatures have one thing in common that makes identifying them as a threat much easier: they're really, really ugly. And they will do ugly things to you if you let them get anywhere near – their toxic excretions alone could leave you paralysed or dead. Or doing their bidding as their mindless slave.

HOW TO SURVIVE A KOUHUN ATTACK

❶ **Prevention is the best approach: make sure your windows and vents are reinforced to prevent someone from cutting through to release kouhuns.**

❷ **Have a security system that will immediately detect any breaches in access points to your dwelling – a breach is concerning not just for what can be removed from living space, but for what can be put in.**

❸ **Install a highly sensitive motion-detector that can detect changes in air pressure from the kouhuns' presence, as they are virtually silent otherwise.**

❹ **It's best you keep a fast-activating melee weapon designed for slicing near you at all times: a lightsaber or vibro-blade. Having a Force-sensitive who can detect danger is always advisable as well.**

HAVE YOU BEEN POISONED?

BITTEN OR STUNG BY CREATURE?

|

PAIN OR NUMBNESS RADIATING FROM WOUND?

|

SUDDEN LACK OF MENTAL FACULTIES?

|

Congratulations, you have been poisoned (and are probably near death)

WHAT ARE KOUHUNS?
Kouhuns are arthropods with many legs jutting beneath a segmented carapace. They can move without making any sound at all and have stingers at their front and back to deliver venom that kills instantly.

⚠ WATCH OUT!

GEONOSIAN BRAIN WORMS

These innocuous-looking nematodes
move with stunning swiftness to enter a
host body's cranial cavity and
take over frontal-lobe
functioning – placing the
victim under their control.

NASAL ENTRY
Access to the brain is
most commonly
achieved through
the nose.

BRAIN INVADERS
Brain worms take control of a host's
cognitive functions, but the worms can be controlled by a
Geonosian queen, who can make the hosts do her bidding

BEWARE!

Many more esoteric threats exist as well, not just
to you but to any pets or animals you may be
hauling and looking to sell – as well as to your
building or starship. Make sure you're insured

ROCK WART
Eight-legged, four-eyed
parasites that use a
neurotoxin to kill prey and
then lay larvae inside their
corpses to incubate.

DURACRETE SLUG
Gnaws through the duracrete
used to construct buildings
and walls, then digests the
material and incorporates
it into its shell.

STONE MITE
Despite the name, these
mostly eat metal and can
use sharp pincers to attach
to starships, using saliva to
eat through the hull.

WORRTS AND ALL
Ugly amphibians that are essentially a
large mouth and larger gullet, worrts can
grow up to 1.5 metres (5 feet) in diameter.
If you're on the smaller side, look out: they
use a rapidly unfurling tongue to catch
unsuspecting creatures that pass by, and
they look so much like rocks you may not
even notice them. Their venom is strong
enough to kill a grown bantha.

INDEX

Page numbers in **bold**
refer to main entries.

Senior Editor David Fentiman
Designers Chris Gould and Jessica Tapolcai
Senior Pre-production Producer Jennifer Murray
Senior Producer Mary Slater
Managing Editor Sadie Smith
Design Manager Vicky Short
Publisher Julie Ferris
Art Director Lisa Lanzarini
Publishing Director Simon Beecroft

DK would like to thank: Brett Rector, Sammy Holland, Michael Siglain, Troy Alders,
Leland Chee, Pablo Hidalgo, Nicole LaCoursiere and Kelly Jensen at Lucasfilm,
Matt Jones for editorial assistance and Elizabeth Dowsett for the index.

First published in Great Britain in 2019 by
Dorling Kindersley Limited
80 Strand, London, WC2R 0RL

Page design copyright © 2019 Dorling Kindersley Limited
A Penguin Random House Company
10 9 8 7 6 5 4 3 2 1
001-309513-Sept/2019

A CIP catalogue record for this book
is available from the British Library.

ISBN: 978-0-24133-133-0

Printed and bound in China

A WORLD OF IDEAS:
SEE ALL THERE IS TO KNOW

www.dk.com
www.starwars.com